Contemporary Irish Writers

Contemporary Irish Writers and Filmmakers

General Series Editor:
Eugene O'Brien, Head of English Department,
Mary Immaculate College, University of Limerick.

Titles in the series:

Seamus Heaney: Creating Irelands of the Mind
by Eugene O'Brien (Mary Immaculate College, Limerick)

Brian Friel: Decoding the Language of the Tribe
by Tony Corbett

Jim Sheridan: Framing the Nation by Ruth Barton
(University College Dublin)

John Banville: Exploring Fictions by Derek Hand
(Dun Laoghaire Institute of Art, Design and Technology)

William Trevor: Re-imagining Ireland by Mary Fitzgerald-Hoyt
(Siena College, New York)

Conor McPherson: Imagining Mischief by Gerald Wood
(Carson-Newman College, Tennessee)

Forthcoming:

Roddy Doyle by Dermot McCarthy

Neil Jordan by Emer Rockett and Kevin Rockett

Jennifer Johnston by Shawn O'Hare

Brian Moore by Philip O'Neill

Maeve Binchy by Kathy Cremin

John McGahern by Eamonn Maher

Colm Toibin by Declan Kiely

Contemporary Irish Writers

John Banville

Exploring Fictions

Derek Hand

The Liffey Press

Published by The Liffey Press
307 Clontarf Road,
Dublin 3, Ireland
www.theliffeypress.com

© 2002 Derek Hand

A catalogue record of this book is
available from the British Library.

ISBN 1-904148-04-2

Front cover photograph © *The Irish Times*.
Reproduced with kind permission.

Printed in the Republic of Ireland by Colorman Ltd.

Contents

About the Author

Derek Hand is currently a Lecturer in English in the Department of Humanities at the Dun Laoghaire Institute of Art, Design and Technology. He was previously Faculty of Arts Fellow in the Department of Anglo-Irish Literature and Drama at University College Dublin. His doctoral thesis dealt with the image of the Anglo-Irish Big House in the work of the poet and dramatist W.B. Yeats, novelist Elizabeth Bowen and contemporary writer John Banville. His main teaching interests are in Irish writing in general, though he has a particular interest in contemporary Irish fiction. He has published numerous articles on Yeats, Banville and aspects of modern Irish fiction. He is a frequent reviewer for *The Irish Times* and *The Sunday Business Post*. He is married and lives in Dublin.

Series Introduction

Given the amount of study that the topic of Irish writing, and increasingly Irish film, has generated, perhaps the first task of a series entitled *Contemporary Irish Writers and Film-makers* is to justify its existence in a time of diminishing rain-forests. As Declan Kiberd's *Irish Classics* has shown, Ireland has produced a great variety of writers who have influenced indigenous, and indeed, world culture, and there are innumerable books devoted to the study of the works of Yeats, Joyce and Beckett. These writers spoke out of a particular Irish culture, and also transcended that culture to speak to the Anglophone world, and beyond.

Ireland, however, has undergone a paradigm shift in the last twenty years. Economically, politically and culturally, it is a vastly different place to the Ireland of Yeats and Joyce. In the light of the fundamentally altered nature of the Diasporic experience, definitions of Irishness and of identity are being rewritten in a more positive light. Irish people now emigrate to well-paid jobs, working in high rise offices in London and New York, a far cry from previous generations whose hard physical labour built those self-same offices. At the same time, the new-found wealth at home has been comple-mented by a growing multiculturalism, challenging perspec-tives on identity like never before.

Modes and worldviews inherited from the past no longer seem adequate to describe an increasingly cosmopolitan and complex society. This is the void which Contemporary Irish Writers and Filmmakers hopes to fill by providing an examination of the state of contemporary cultural Ireland through an analysis of its writers and filmmakers.

The role of the aesthetic in the shaping of attitudes and opinions cannot be understated and these books will attempt to understand the transformative potential of the work of the artist in the context of the ongoing redefinition of society and culture. The current proliferation of writers and filmmakers of the highest quality can be taken as an index of the growing confidence of this society, and in the desire to enunciate that confidence. However, as Luke Gibbons has put it: "a people has not found its voice until it has expressed itself, not only in a body of creative works, but also in a body of critical works," and Contemporary Irish Writers and Filmmakers is part of such an attempt to find that voice.

Aimed at the student and general reader alike, this series will analyse and examine the major texts, themes and topics that have been addressed by these present-day voices. At another level, each book will trace the effect of a specific artist on the mindset of Irish people.

It is hoped that this series will encourage discussion and debate about issues that have engaged the writers and filmmakers who enunciate, and transform, contemporary Irish culture. It is further hoped that the series will play its part in enabling our continuing participation in the great humanistic project of understanding ourselves and others.

Eugene O'Brien
Department of English
Mary Immaculate College
University of Limerick

Acknowledgements

My interest in the work of John Banville goes back many years. During that time, it has been my good fortune to have had many friends and colleagues who have been of enormous help and encouragement in furthering that interest. Declan Kiberd and Tony Roche from the Department of Anglo-Irish Literature and Drama in UCD have been both teachers and colleagues of mine for many years and their help has been truly and especially sustaining. I would also like to mention former colleagues from that Department, Brian Donnelly, Caitriona Clutterbuck, Frank McGuinness and Jeff Holdridge. I would like to thank Anne Fogarty for her many words and gestures of encouragement and for being a kind taskmaster in her role as director of the James Joyce Summer School. From the Mater Dei Institute, I would like to acknowledge John Devitt and Brendan McDonnell. From the Department of Humanities in the Dun Laoghaire Institute of Art, Design and Technology, I would like to mention Eithne Guilfoyle and Josephine Browne.

There are many who share my interest in John Banville but I would I like to single out Hedwig Schwall and Elke d'Hoker from Leuven in Belgium, in particular, for sharing their ideas with me; and, of course, John Kenny from Galway. Also, my cousin Michael Hand who still possesses a keen interest in Irish fiction and in John Banville especially. P.J. Mathews and Beth Wightman are two fellow students of Irish Studies with whom I have had a friendship for what seems like forever; their presence and encouragement has been invaluable. I would like also to mention Fionnuala Hanrahan from the Wexford County Library, for inviting me to give a series of seminars on John Banville in Enniscorthy in early 2001. These gatherings brought together a diverse group of people who challenged me to explain my ideas and thoughts, and for that I am grateful.

The general editor of this series, Eugene O'Brien, has been a great source of inspiration and help and, along with Brian Langan from The Liffey Press, got me through some difficult moments during the past year with patience and understanding.

My mother and my brother Brian have been, without knowing it, a tremendous source of strength. Thank you.

Finally, to Paula, who has always believed in me with this project and in every other project I have undertaken. This book could not have come into being without you.

Derek Hand
Killester, Dublin
February 2002

In Memory of my Father
Jim Hand 1937–2001

Chronology

1945	John Banville born in Wexford on 8 December to Martin and Agnes (Doran) Banville. He has one brother, Vincent, and one sister, Vonnie. He is educated by the Christian Brothers and at St. Peter's College, Wexford.
1965	First short story, "The Party", to be published in *Kilkenny Magazine*.
1966	Second short story, "A Death", to be published in *Kilkenny Magazine*.
1967	Wins Allied Irish Banks and Irish-America Foundation Literary Award.
1969	Becomes copy-editor for *The Irish Press*. Marries Janet Dunham. They have two children.
1970	*Long Lankin* published.
1971	*Nightspawn* published.
1973	*Birchwood* published. Macaulay Fellowship of Irish Arts Council.

1976	*Doctor Copernicus* published. Wins Whitbread Prize and James Tait Black Memorial Prize.
1981	*Kepler* published. Wins Guardian Prize for Fiction.
1982	*The Newton Letter* published.
1983	Leaves *Irish Press* to devote himself more fully to his writing.
1984	*Reflections*, a cinematic adaptation of *The Newton Letter*, is broadcast on Britain's Channel Four, with a screenplay by John Banville and starring Gabriel Byrne. Becomes member of Aosdána.
1986	*Mefisto* published. Joins *Irish Times* as sub-editor.
1988	Becomes Literary Editor of *The Irish Times*.
1989	*The Book of Evidence* published. Short-listed for the Booker Prize. Winner of the Guinness Peat Aviation Literary Award.
1993	*Ghosts* published.
1994	*The Broken Jug* performed in the Peacock Theatre, Dublin. *Seachange* broadcast on RTE television.
1995	*Athena* published.
1997	*The Untouchable* published. Wins Lannan Literary Award.
1999	Adapts Elizabeth Bowen's Big House novel *The Last September* for screen.
2000	*Eclipse* published. *God's Gift* performed at the Dublin Theatre Festival in October.
2002	Resigns from Aosdána.

List of Abbreviations

Chapter One

Introduction: John Banville, Irish Modernism and Postmodernism

That last elusive word, the stammerer's obsession,
that surely would make all come marvellously clear
— (*DC*, 63)

John Banville's artistic achievement is such that, while he has been telling the same story for many years, he has been able to make something fresh and original of his modernist and postmodernist concerns again and again. The story he tells is one in which his protagonists come to understand the limitations of the human imagination's engagement with the real world. All of his writing is an attempt to delineate this strain and tension at the heart of the modern condition. It is a crisis permeating all levels of his characters' experience and existence, so that the reality of self, others, the world, are questioned and interrogated.

There are variations on this basic tale, but it is the same story nonetheless. These concerns can be broadly labelled as postmodern and, indeed, some of Banville's foremost critics see him as a universal/international writer dealing with general post-enlightenment themes of dissolution, deflation, deconstruction, and distrust. It is far too easy, however, to label Banville and his work as simply and straightforwardly "postmodern".

Terms like postmodernism and modernism are confusing and unstable. Certainly there is no accepted understanding of these terms among cultural commentators, philosophers and literary critics. It is not my intention here to get bogged down in any ongoing debate about their meaning and, indeed, their relevance or worth to discussing works of literature. As a key to understanding Banville's aesthetic sensibility, though, brief and very simplified working definitions are necessary.

Irish philosopher Richard Kearney declares that the modern imagination is a productive one:

> to cite the canonical metaphor, the imagination ceases to function as a mirror reflecting some external reality and becomes a lamp which projects its own internally generated light onto things. As a consequence of this momentous reversal of roles, meaning is no longer primarily considered as a transcendent property of divine being; it is now hailed as a transcendental product of the human mind. (Kearney, 1988a: 155)

In a fragmented and apparently chaotic world, the modernist artist imposes meaning and order upon the world. The modernist writer believes that by being "new" and experimentally original, a connection can be made with reality, and that the world can be said in words.

On the other hand, the postmodern imagination is parodic rather than productive and is typified by the metaphor of a looking-glass:

> or to be more precise, of an interplay between multiple looking glasses which reflect each other interminably. The postmodern paradigm is, in other words, that of a labyrinth of mirrors which extend

> infinitely in all directions a labyrinth where the image
> of the self (as presence to itself) dissolves into self-
> parody. (Kearney, 1988a: 253)

There is no hidden order or meaning: all is but a "mirroring which mirrors nothing but the act of mirroring" (Kearney, 1988a: 254–5). The postmodern writer supposedly confronts a meaningless world with an almost flippant shrug of the shoulder: it does not matter because nothing matters or means anything anymore. In the place of purposeful meaning and significance is a playful, anti-hierarchical openness (Hassan, 1982: 267–8). In its determination to break with the unifying and all-encompassing ideas associated with modernism, postmodernism is understood by some to be a philosophy concerned with freedom. All aspects of life and culture are placed in inverted commas — "reality", "meaning", "art" — and in the process made ironic. Postmodernity, perhaps, might be best thought of as a "mood" — a kind of mocking, perhaps even cynical, certainly a "knowing" pose or attitude — rather than anything categorically definite (Docherty, 1993: 1–31).

While John Banville's writing does indeed concern itself with these postmodern issues and certainly displays postmodern tendencies and techniques, it is better and more suitable to consider his art as oscillating between a modernist and a postmodernist perspective. Unlike other so-called postmodern writers, his is not a work that views the contemporary postmodern moment where the free-play of language reigns supreme as a liberated and liberating situation. Joseph McMinn puts it best when considering Linda Hutcheon's attempt to defend postmodernist art, and thus Banville's writing, as a "kind of fictional liberation movement". McMinn recognises that such a reading of Banville fails to register "the deep sense of critical sympathy in Banville for those . . . who dreamed of metanarratives and unifying visions":

> Banville can deconstruct with the best of them, but there is never the feeling in his work that the exposure of constructed myths about identity and nature is a simple cause for celebration. Quite the opposite . . . There may no longer be any hope of a convincing master narrative, but most of Banville's characters wish there were. (McMinn, 1999: 7)

Such a position of being caught between hope and despair, of being enthralled by the prospect of saying the world while simultaneously admitting the futility of any such act of saying actually connecting with the world, is fundamentally central to any understanding of John Banville's art.

As a result, what marks off Banville's fiction from that of other postmodern writers in the contemporary moment is that he feels deeply the loss of those grand narratives that explained the world and our place in the world. Coupled with this is a remaining sense of hope that perhaps this rupture in the human imagination's relationship with the world can be healed. His is an art concerned with attempting to overcome the postmodern rift between language and experience, fiction and reality. It is this yearning that ensures that Banville will continue to write in the hope that the next word, the next paragraph, the next story will surely make "all come marvellously clear" (*DC*, 63).

While these concerns with the nature of language, the imagination, art and the reality they connect with and supposedly map are highly pertinent to western thought and culture in general, they also possess a particular and peculiar resonance in a specifically Irish context. It is important to consider Banville's relationship to the "matter of Ireland" and how it informs his work as a whole. By doing so, it is possible to begin to understand some of the motivations behind his fiction and why certain themes, obsessions and images are returned to over and over again in his writing. It is important also that in a series such as the present one, an attempt is made to highlight the major questions and issues that concern Irish writing and culture in general. What follows, then, is a brief summary of some of those issues and Banville's connection to them.

John Banville himself has repeatedly downplayed the importance of his being Irish to engaging with his work: "I stay in this country but I'm not going to be an Irish writer. I'm not going to do the Irish thing" (Schwall, 1997: 19). It is difficult to ascertain what exactly the author intends with this remark. There can be no question that Banville's work differs greatly from the majority of Irish writing of the contemporary moment,[1] but to declare, then, that it is not "Irish" or that it eschews "Irish" themes and concerns is too easy and convenient a move on the author's part. Perhaps Banville has been influenced by one of his foremost critics, Rüdiger Imhof.

Imhof, very clearly and concisely, frames John Banville's work in a European/international setting, believing the Ireland of his art is merely a convenient backdrop to the more serious and interesting postmodern concerns being dealt with in the foreground. It is worth considering Imhof's critical evaluation of Banville's particular position in relation to Irish literature in general:

---

[1] In a recent survey study of contemporary Irish fiction, Gerry Smyth's *The Novel and the Nation: Studies in the New Irish Fiction* (1997, London: Pluto Press), there is no sustained evaluation of Banville's work, while almost every other writer of the last 15 years has at least one book considered. To be fair, Smyth acknowledges this lacuna in his introduction. Yet, it serves to highlight how difficult it is to categorise Banville's writing with reference to Irish writing/literature in general.

Irish fiction in the twentieth century has been quite
conventional in subject matter and technique, despite Joyce and Beckett and in spite of what has been
going on elsewhere in the world. Too much is about
Ireland, the sow that eats her farrow, about a priest-
ridden God-forsaken race . . . Too much is in the
mould of cosy realism. The exceptions are too few
and far between. The . . . [second generation] writers . . . are fundamentally ploughing the same clod of
clay that the first generation of twentieth-century
Irish writers toiled over — writers who, by undivid-
edly concentrating on matters intrinsically Irish, were
concerned with helping to find a national identity.
Now that this identity is found, one could reasonably
expect an opening up of the focus of interest. Such
an opening up has still to be accomplished on a larger scale. Banville has shown himself to be among
the very few who have sought to attain this goal . . .
[H]e has turned to incontestably non-Irish subject
matter. As a result, some regard him as the black
sheep in the family of Irish writers; others, strangely
enough, think he is not a typical Irish writer at all, for
whatever that may be worth. (Imhof, 1997: 7)

While Imhof's remarks are focused on the art of Banville,
they depend on a reading of Irish literature and culture that
is highly questionable and yet still pervasive in Irish studies. It
is worthwhile, therefore, giving some time to contemplating
Imhof's estimation of Irish writing.[2]

Firstly, it is more accurate to say that *most* writing fails
to take up where James Joyce and Samuel Beckett left off.
The majority of writing today is "conventional" and tradi-

---

[2] In engaging with Rüdiger Imhof in this manner I do not intend to
diminish Imhof's importance and centrality to Banville studies.
Rather, I want to highlight one area where his reading and interpretation is seriously flawed.

tional, presenting itself in the mould of "cosy realism". It is as if the vistas opened up by Joyce and Beckett are too terrible to contemplate and writers — everywhere — retreat in the face of such formalistic and thematic experimentation. It is unfair, consequently, to single out Irish writing as having failed to learn the lessons of Joyce and Beckett, when almost everyone else has too.

More important, however, is how Imhof buys into a "progress/backwardness" dichotomy in his reading of Irish history and culture. Those writers and artists involved in the literary revival were — in Imhof's estimation (this is implied, of course, and not overtly stated) — caught up in something other than "modernity" in their concentration on only Irish themes and concerns. He feels that Irish writers need to look to new themes, that they need to break out of their too narrow focus and become open to fresh experiences. The language here, when one analyses it, is very prejudicial. Imhof talks of "opening up", which implies its negative opposite — constraint, lack of freedom and so on. Even Imhof's rhetoric underlines his view of the contemporary Irish scene. His playful comment, for example, about how Irish writers are "ploughing the same clod of clay" over and over again upholds the progress/backwardness template by patronisingly underpinning his thoughts in reference to "rural" language. Thus, Irish writers — figuratively at least — are to be connected with the rural scene, an anti-modern place in comparison to the modernity of Europe (and the rest of the world) which looks "forward", and not "backward" as in Ireland.

Ultimately, Rüdiger Imhof is perpetuating one of the hoariest of stereotypes applied to Ireland and things Irish: that it is a place of backwardness and narrow-mindedness. But it has ever been thus with Irish writers in the eyes of some commentators: the more "modern" and forward-looking Irish artists are, the less Irish they become.[3] On one level, it could be said that such a stance is setting up a dichotomy between the "past" and the "future": those engaged in "traditional" forms of writing are caught in the past; while those who adhere to this "anti-traditional" or "modern" stance embrace the future. Another way of putting this is that those who see themselves as fundamentally opposed to the traditional perceive themselves as being above the supposed "backwardness" and "narrowness" of Irish writing and culture.

Perhaps the most disturbing implication inherent in Imhof's remarks is that Ireland and Irish writing are fundamentally at odds with the general movement and thrust of what is going on, supposedly, everywhere else. In this reading, Ireland and Irish culture has nothing to offer and instead must "take" its lead from others and other cultures. Ireland, thus, does not create culture; it only reflects and imitates trends from the wider, and more authoritative, European/ international arena. Surprisingly, Imhof reinscribes and reinforces the quite unpostmodern concept of the centre, with Ireland very much on the periphery.

Even more disturbing is the sense that, if one follows the above argument to its logical conclusion, the issues being dealt with by modernist/postmodernist writers and artists have nothing to connect them with the Irish experience. Thus, the problem no longer simply centres round Irish themes and Irish subject matter being "backward"; rather,

---

[3] Writers such as James Joyce and Samuel Beckett, for example — because they engage with modernity — do so at the expense of their "Irishness". And, of course, both lived outside Ireland, their physical apartness from Ireland signalling their inability to exist in such a narrow and backward place. It is a neat picture of how Irish writing works and is very popular. However, it is far too simplistic and, while adhering to a stereotypical view of Ireland, it also does not allow for the actual complexity of the Irish experience.

the problem is reformulated as one of Ireland being outside, and cut off from, the accepted development of European/ Western culture. Basically, to be Irish and modern/post-modern is an impossibility; they are mutually exclusive concepts. Consequently, questions concerning language, the self, reality, being, knowledge, are not relevant in an Irish context and have nothing to say about the Irish condition; and, in turn, the Irish condition has nothing to say concerning the wider human condition.

Richard Kearney argues that, in the twentieth century, Ireland has witnessed what he calls a "crisis of culture":

> This has often been experienced as a conflict be-tween the claims of tradition and modernity. Such an experience of residing between two worlds — one dying, the other struggling to be born — has given rise in turn to a crisis of consciousness. How is one to confront the pervading sense of discontinuity, the absence of a coherent identity, the breakdown of in-herent ideologies and beliefs, the insecurities of fragmentation? Is it possible to make the transition between past and future, between that which is fa-miliar to us and that which is foreign? (Kearney, 1988b: 9)

Kearney's estimation of the Irish situation firmly places Ireland and Irish writing in a "modern" or "modernist" context because what he is describing is the predicament that confronts all writers and thinkers in this century, and not simply in Ire-land, of how to negotiate between the past and the future, through the present. His further argument, that this tension between what in the Irish situation is called "revivalist" writing and its supposed opposite "modernist" writing must be both thought of overall in terms of modernism, is crucial. Impor-tantly, Kearney undermines the simple sentiment of the backwardness/progress model of Irish studies, recognising that the impetus behind the revivalist movement is an un-equivocally modern one, despite its overt claims to tradition and traditional culture (Kearney, 1988b: 10–16). It is here, perhaps, that Ireland's post-colonial status can be observed to complicate the issue in that terms like "progress", "moder-nity", "tradition", can possess a different resonance to that in which they are used elsewhere. Thus, rather than thinking in terms of "Ireland/Irishness" and "modernity" as being mutu-ally exclusive, it is more accurate to say that the Irish experi-ence is fundamentally modern because essential to the Irish condition is this notion of transition. In other words: we are modern because we are Irish, not in spite of it.

Kearney argues that modernism in an Irish context can be described in many ways: "revivalist modernism", "radical-ist modernism" and "mediational modernism". This last term he prefers to label postmodernism in that it cannot, in Kear-ney's words, "strictly be confined to either modernist or revivalist categories" (Kearney, 1988b: 14). Underpinning each conception is this idea of transition: of moving, or try-ing to move, between opposing positions, and self-reflexively questioning those opposing positions. However, it is post-modernism that truly encapsulates this "transitional" para-digm.

John Banville's position of being caught between a mod-ern and a postmodern perspective — both he and his char-acters wavering between desiring order and meaning while simultaneously recognising its absence, both looking forward and backward at the same time — would seem to corre-spond to Richard Kearney's concept of postmodernism in an Irish context as "mediational modernism". Again, perhaps the Irish post-colonial context is an unconscious influence here: the colonised distrusting the master codes being thrust upon them by the coloniser while simultaneously lamenting the loss of their own narrative and desiring to construct a new narrative of their own.

Accepting Richard Kearney's model for Irish studies allows us to begin to place John Banville in an Irish context. Imhof, while acknowledging Kearney's contribution to the appraisal of post-Joycean fiction in Ireland, chastises him, erroneously, for believing that the "critical fiction" practised by writers such as Banville is a purely "indigenous Irish phenomenon". Imhof goes on to underline, yet again, the "international" provenance of such fiction, and such sensibilities in fiction, dismissing any relevance to Ireland and Irishness (Imhof, 1997: 9–10). Of course, his attack on Kearney is unfair because Kearney is not claiming exclusivity for the Irish condition, but is rather highlighting very clearly how Irish writing participates in the concerns of the wider international community in a way that Imhof is unable to admit, or condone. Indeed, Kearney's highlighting of the concept of "transition" stresses exchange, intercourse and interconnection — intellectual, literary and cultural — between Ireland and a wider community; and, crucially, does not privilege any one position in this equation: thus, Ireland can take ideas from elsewhere, but it can also, importantly, offer ideas and theories to the wider world.

Though Kearney is not making claims for Ireland's exclusivity in terms of the modern/postmodern novel or modernity/postmodernity in general, he is subtly offering an opinion that, perhaps, these concerns — shared by most western cultures and communities — are thrown into sharp relief in the Irish situation.[4] Reading Banville's work can certainly make us aware of this possibility.

John Banville has stated that every contemporary Irish writer has to take one of two aesthetic directions: to follow either the path of James Joyce or of Samuel Beckett. It is, for him, a necessarily stark choice. He very pointedly and force-

---

[4] This could be one reason for the continuing growth in interest in Irish writing and Irish culture.

fully opts to acknowledge Samuel Beckett as his literary forebear (Schwall, 1997: 17). However, as was the case with his modernist and/or postmodernist tendencies, and his position as regards Irish writing, it is fair to contend that such clear-cut, unambiguous statements by either the author himself or some of his critics are not wholly reliable. It is possible, despite his own vehement assertions to the contrary, to productively conceive of Banville as being the true inheritor of two distinct Irish literary traditions represented by James Joyce on the one hand and Samuel Beckett on the other.

James Joyce's experimentation as a novelist is obviously crucial. Modernist fiction in the early twentieth century hoped to reformulate the novel in order that it connect with reality in ways that the nineteenth-century novel could not. In consequence, the happy consensus between narrator and reader — so very much central to nineteenth-century fiction — is abandoned in favour of disorientating techniques designed to force the reader to engage with the novel's rendering of reality in new ways. Joyce, of course, surpasses most other modernist writers in his efforts to stretch the novel form to its very limits.

In a specifically Irish context, it has been argued that Joyce's "realism" is important because his very act of writing, his very act of imagining, the reality of an Irish world, is an act of rebellion (Deane, 1985: 92–107). Ireland's colonial and post-colonial status means that "reality" is a problematical category in terms of whose version of reality is being represented (Brown, 1991: 159–73). Put simply, Joyce's attempt to get "everything in" is an act of empowerment on his behalf as an author. Banville's writing, too, is concerned with reality and the world: his interrogative and experimental fictions are important in the contemporary moment because they force his readers to ask similar questions to those thrown up by Joyce's texts.

James Joyce is important to Irish writing also because of his works' single-minded focus on and celebration of the intellect and the imagination (Deane, 1985: 75–91). In a country where the stereotype was one where the Irish laboured with the "despotism of fact", such a representation of the Irish character can never be underestimated. This is also very true of John Banville's writing. More than any other Irish writer in the contemporary moment, Banville has carved out a unique niche for himself, allowing him the opportunity to meditate on the nature of the artistic and creative imagination. All of his characters, from Nicholas Copernicus to Freddie Montgomery, are shown thinking and intellectualising about their place in the world and about their relationship to it, so much so that in many of his books it is very obvious that story is not hugely important to him. It is one of the main reasons that his work is challenging for many readers, as Joyce's was before him. He is at times more concerned with concepts than with plot and thus his are books about and of ideas.

While it can be said that Banville is influenced by Joyce and his work, it is a negative influence in terms of his own art. He has declared himself to be a "survivor of Joyce" in that he, like so many other writers in the contemporary moment, in acknowledging what Joyce achieved, are unable to persevere in his wake (Banville, 1990: 73–81). It is as if that belief, that power and authority, that sustained Joyce is no longer possible in the world we now inhabit. Thus, Banville has himself on numerous occasions declared that his own art follows the path of Samuel Beckett.

Beckett's is an art of an almost heroic, certainly stoic, failure. After the artistic sure-footedness of high modernism epitomised by Joyce, the experimental impulse moved inwards and began questioning the actual possibility of creating or saying anything. A very helpful and straightforward distinction between modernist and postmodernist writing is made by literary critic Brian McHale. The former, he argues, is concerned with epistemological issues; that is to say, modernism foregrounds the intellect and the imagination and how it apprehends the world about it. Postmodern writing, he goes on to say, is concerned with ontological issues: in other words, questions of Being — of what it is to exist (McHale, 1987: 59–72). The opening lines of Banville's novel *Birchwood* encapsulate this shift: "I am, therefore I think" (*BW*, 11). In this playful reversal of seventeenth-century philosopher Rene Descartes' famous dictum, Being is privileged above conscious Being.

Such a shift also signals a self-reflexive consideration of the ontological status of the text itself. Thus, the act of writing is questioned and its relationship to the "real" world probed. All of Banville's novels are books about the writing of books. All of his characters struggle with telling their stories, if not through the act of writing, then simply in the telling itself. It must be stressed that while this is a central aspect of his work, unlike other postmodern writing, it is raised to a level far beyond cliché.

One particular quotation from Samuel Beckett sums up concisely his literary philosophy in the post-Joycean world of writing. Beckett asserts his artistic impotence in this way: "there is nothing to express, nothing with which to express, no power to express. No desire to express, together with the obligation to express" (Beckett, 1970: 103).

So, while at the heart of Joyce's writing is an idea of power, at the centre of Beckett's is powerlessness. This loss of power is coupled with a desire to "say" or create in the manner that Joyce and other modernists were able to say and create. It is a paradoxical and contradictory predicament best encapsulated in another more famous line from Beckett: "I can't go on, I'll go on" (Beckett, 1979: 382).

Just as Joyce's situation of coming from an increasingly upwardly mobile Catholic middle class informs his work of empowerment,[5] Beckett's position as an Anglo-Irish Protestant whose elite social and economic situation is constantly under threat in twentieth-century Ireland is a crucial factor in his art of powerlessness. Whereas Joyce desires to, and is able to, imagine a community — however dysfunctional — in his wonderful rendering of myriad voices in his work, Beckett increasingly retreats toward the singular voice, very alone and cut off from the possibility of any redemptive interaction with others. Banville too places solitary narrators centre stage, attempting to make sense of themselves in relation to other people in their world.

John Banville, then, very consciously inherits these twin traditions of Irish writing and Irish society, as represented by James Joyce and Samuel Beckett. All of this is argued, of course, in direct opposition to Banville's own stated beliefs on this subject. Yet it is interesting to note that in many of his "Irish" novels, he plays with this duel inheritance very openly by his having his characters caught between Anglo-Irish and Gaelic traditions. He recognises the hybridity or duality at the heart of the contemporary Irish psyche and works with the consequent strain that this produces.

Underlining this is how Banville's novels abound with dualities, tense opposites and anxious disjunctions. His focus on language and the slipperiness of the written word, for instance, can be understood as a manifestation of the tension between a Gaelic oral tradition and an Anglo-Irish written tradition. In a talk delivered in 1980, Banville clearly acknowledges the post-colonial predicament with language in the Irish situation:

---

[5] Though, of course, Joyce's own family history is one of a long spiral into economic hardship and debt, it can still be argued that culturally he remains part of this new middle class.

> The imposition of English, a pragmatic and rational tool, upon the grid of Irish speech rhythms, and, more important perhaps, upon the peculiarly oblique Irish sensibility, resulted in a language at once wonderfully expressive and . . . poetically imprecise. . . . For the Irish, language is not primarily a tool for expressing what we mean. Sometimes I think it is quite the opposite. We have profound misgivings about words. We love them . . . but we do not trust them. (Banville, 1981: 14)

He goes on to argue that he is not interested in resurrecting stereotypical images of Irish people being unable to conform to the despotism of fact and asserts that his interest is in showing how "subversive, destructive even" is the Irish use of the English language (Banville, 1981: 14). Thus, Banville — the postmodern writer — is aware that in the contemporary moment, language is problematical but he also admits that there is an added significance to that distrust in the Irish context and that it must be acknowledged and attended to. A question, therefore, constantly being raised in Banville's writing is, if language is the way we see the world, communicate the world to others, live in the world, and make the world our own, what happens if that language is inadequate? Another question then poses itself: what happens if that language is someone else's? In other words, Banville is accepting that Hiberno-English is, essentially, a language with uncertainty at its core and thus the perfect medium — for him — through which to articulate his postmodern concerns.

Indeed, it can be argued that many of the conditions that we now accept as modern and postmodern have been fundamental to any notion of Irishness or Irish identity in, certainly, the last two hundred years. For instance, when Ferdinand de Saussure began to question the relationship between the signifier and the signified in the early part of the twentieth century, and forever undermined language's relationship to reality, his discovery would not have been wholly surprising, or particularly shattering, to an Irish person. The loss (or jettisoning) of the Irish language in nineteenth-century Ireland and the simultaneous acquisition of the English language, produces a situation — still palpable in contemporary Ireland — of moving between two worlds articulated in either language but never being entirely at home in either. In other words, the conclusion that perhaps language is not the "clear lens" that it was once thought to be, is an essentially inherent feature of the Irish condition.

It should not be thought therefore that Banville dismisses words and their worth. Rather, what can be observed in his writing is a poetic sensibility toward language and its nuances. He is known to obsessively rewrite paragraphs and whole sections of his work in order to achieve the correct timbre and tone (Brown, 1991: 171). The effects are often startling, with descriptions of the everyday detritus of life transformed into moments of intense reality plucked from the incessant drift of existence. Yet, even as Banville so expertly and deftly renders the world in words, such moments in their profound clarity, and indeed because of that clarity, call attention to themselves precisely as representations. The reader will notice, too, that Banville has a tendency to interrupt his narrative on occasions to muse self-consciously on words or phrases, and their application to the world of lived experience. For instance, his character Freddie Montgomery in *The Book of Evidence* talks about his "getting life" as punishment for his crime, realising that this well-worn phrase does not connect with the reality of his situation. There is hope and despair here — hope that a language adequate to the predicament of living can be created, but despair also in recognising that such a language may never be attainable.

His concerns can also be discerned at the level of form. In his early work, especially, he can be seen to be preoccupied with the form of the novel, testing its limits and experimenting with how he presents his material. The kind of coherence and chronological development that we might expect from a novel are, at times, wholly absent in his work. That type of stability presupposes a resolution to problems, both individual and social, that Banville wants to deny in his work. Dilemmas are, for Banville, ongoing and his dealing with them is a process rather than a solution. The resulting instability is a reflection of how genres and forms from elsewhere must be moulded and shaped to the peculiarities of the Irish experience.

Anxiety and uncertainty, then, permeate the Irish experience and are registered in Banville's writing both formally and linguistically. However, it is not only in the area of language and form that the strains of duality can be observed. His Irish novels, as has been stated, feature characters and situations that exploit this double legacy of been positioned in the hyphenated space between Anglo and Irish. All his characters, though, experience a sense of fracture and incompleteness. Banville constantly employs the motif of twins or the double in his work, making his concerns with this idea of rupture and disconnection — in its various manifestations — tangible.

Realising that Banville has a relationship to Irish writing and culture is important for comprehending his own singular approach to creating fiction in the contemporary moment. My argument is that his radical "in-betweenness" — his being neither a Joycean modernist nor a Beckettian postmodernist but an amalgamation of both; his desiring a word or words that can grasp the real, yet simultaneously despairing that such a language is possible; his many characters' relentless search for a true authentic self that always ends with the pessimistic conclusion that aching hollowness is perhaps all there is — is best understood within an Irish context. For Irish culture and Irish writing has constantly attempted to redefine itself on its own terms and at an angle to main-stream cultures and literature. In doing so, it could be said, the hoped-for result is not an exclusive idea of Ireland or sense of Irishness, but perhaps a simple explication of being human. In a country that is obsessed, and has been for a long time, with who we are and what other people think we are, it has been sometimes forgotten that to be Irish is to be human also, even if that humanity is necessarily coloured by local conditions. Maybe what Banville is investigating is how the individual operates or exists in relation to a wider com-munity. His consistent focus on the single voice or con-sciousness trying to make sense of themselves in the world highlights that, even in a postmodern and post-nationalist Ireland, identity is still an unresolved issue.

Perhaps, though, Banville's Irishness is to be found in his insistence on the transformative nature of art and the artis-tic imagination. In other words, for Banville, as for so many Irish writers of the past, art can actually matter in the real political world of intervention and change. It could be ar-gued, for instance, that his science tetralogy, begun in the 1970s, is a retreat from that reality. How better to escape the horrors of violence in the North of Ireland than to re-treat into the middle ages and consider the lives of historical figures such as Copernicus and Kepler? And yet these nov-els, with their focus on the imagination and its potential, and their experimentation with the form of the novel itself, force readers to look again at the world, to consider again how we live in the world and how we live with others — even enemies — in that world. For Banville, the purpose of art is not to tell it as it is, but rather to imagine it as it might be. He is fond of quoting from the poet Rainer Maria Rilke's *Dunio Elegies*:

> . . . Are we, perhaps, here just for saying: House.
> Bridge, Fountain, Gate, Jug, Fruit tree, Window,

possibly: Pillar, Tower? But for saying, remember,
oh, for such saying as never the things themselves
hoped so intensely to be. (Banville, 1981: 15)

The very act of saying transfigures the world about us, offers
hope of change in the face of the hard facts of reality. It has
always been thus in Ireland. Our truly great writers like Oscar Wilde, W.B. Yeats and James Joyce have used their art in
order that a better world could be imagined; and if imagined,
might in time actually come to be. Such imagining is an ongoing project and it is my belief that John Banville is fully engaged in that project. As he said himself recently: "We do
love a dreamer" (Banville, 2001: 13).

   This present study cannot hope to deal adequately with
all of John Banville's writing. Since 1970, he has produced
twelve novels, two plays, a short film for television, as well
as short stories. Such an output is a great achievement, especially when it is acknowledged that there is a coherent
aesthetic binding this body of work together. Rather than
attempting to cover each text in full, I propose to consider a
selection of his work grouped together thematically. Thus,
the novels *Birchwood* and *The Newton Letter* will be considered under the heading of "Irish matters". These two works,
in particular, engage with the notion of history and the past
in an Irish context. He is not simply concerned with showing
his readers the past; he wants also to show how the past is
created in the present and is mediated to us through writing
and myth. Two novels from his science tetralogy, *Doctor
Copernicus* and *Kepler*, will be discussed in terms of their self-
reflexive meditation on the nature of art and the artistic
imagination. All of Banville's writing is self-conscious, in that
he demonstrates quite clearly the process of writing itself,
and indeed his work considered collectively can be thought
of as a long conversation with himself as an author ponder-
ing the delicate balance between the world and art's connec-

tion with that world. These first two chapters will offer close readings of the texts being discussed. It is a necessary and potentially fruitful task because Banville's texts respond well to such in-depth scrutiny and should set a solid basis of understanding for the final chapter. In that chapter *Mefisto*, *The Book of Evidence*, *Ghosts*, *The Untouchable* and *Eclipse* will be examined as novels that have moved their focus inwards toward an investigation of the self. The choice of texts is certainly personal, but they are also representative of his output in general and should aid any reader in coming to grips with his other work, and indeed, future work. It must also be said that, inevitably, there is much cross-over between these thematic groupings and they should not be thought of as in any way rigid or definitive. Banville's abilities mean that his major concerns are returned to in each of his novels and what can be said of one could, in truth, be said of all.

Chapter Two

Birchwood and *The Newton Letter:*
Awakening from the Nightmare of
Irish History

It is not the literal past, the "facts" of history, that
shape us, but images of the past embodied in language . . . We must never cease renewing those images; because once we do, we fossilize. (Brian Friel,
1989: 445)

The one duty we owe to history is to rewrite it.
(Oscar Wilde, 1983: 1,023)

James Joyce in his great novel *Ulysses* has his character Stephen Dedalus declare: "History . . . is a nightmare from
which I am trying to awake" (Joyce, 1991: 42). Many commentators on Joyce's work interpret this statement as referring to Irish history in particular. Stephen's difficulty is that
he feels, in an Irish context, that history is a burden and cannot be escaped. The Ireland of 1904 is too much concerned
with the rights and wrongs of the past than with confronting
the issues of the present and the possibilities of the future.
There is a hint of determinism here too: that, because of this

problem with the past, with history, Ireland's collective future is somehow fated — and not, obviously, in any positive
way. For the character Dedalus and the author Joyce, it is a
case of having to flee a backward Ireland in order to enter
into a more progressive and productive universalism.

The implications of Dedalus's statement are far-reaching
because this escape/entrapment paradigm has become something of a model for engaging with and understanding Irish
writing and culture as a whole. In this reading, the choice
being offered is a decidedly stark one: either escape Ireland
and Irish history or be forever trapped by its supposedly
obsessive backward look. It is this kind of thinking that underpins many of the debates surrounding Irish culture's relationship to tradition and modernity where, as was argued in
the introduction, the choices are presented in simple "ei-
ther/or" terms.

In Irish life and culture, this has led to a constant debate
— battle even — concerning the past and its significance in
the present. In the contemporary moment, much of this debate revolves round the issue of "revisionism" versus na-
tionalism in historical and literary studies. Revisionist historians, especially, have seen themselves as "opening up" Irish
history in order to get beyond the narrow, reductive and
backward — as they see it — nationalist history that is supposedly the "nightmare" that Stephen Dedalus talks of. Na-
tionalism's tendency toward a heroic narrative is undermined in the general demythologising project undertaken by
Irish revisionist historians. Myth, adventure and romance are
to be replaced by dispassionate objectivity — that is to say,
the facts — presented without bias or prejudice. This debate
is not simply confined to academic circles. In Ireland, this
project has become, in popular terms, an act of wilful amnesia. In a desperate desire to engage with modernity, some
actively promote a position of forgetting ourselves — of cut-

ting ourselves off from the past — in order that a metro-politan future can be gained.

Is such national amnesia possible or, indeed, worthwhile? The Anglo-Irish writer Elizabeth Bowen neatly summed up the predicament in a piece written for the British Ministry of Information from Ireland during the Second World War: "I could wish that the English kept history in mind more [and] that the Irish kept it in mind less" (Fisk, 1983: 356).

The sense, on the Irish side, is of being "stuck", unable to move on, debilitated and held back. And yet, crucially, Bowen recognises that there is a loss of a kind in Britain's position to and with history — that "amnesia" concerning the past and history is not necessarily a more positive state of existence. Importantly, she is looking for some sort of balance that will allow a proper movement from the past, through the present and on into the future. For the debate is not so much about the past as the future and how to have a productive engagement with the possibilities and potential that the future might have in store.

Certainly, John Banville's work can be seen to respond to and confront these issues. His career in writing, especially in the 1970s and the 1980s, has coincided with the emergence of these major debates in Irish culture. As was argued in the Introduction, many critics and commentators of his work would perceive him as escaping, in a Joycean and Beckettian tradition, the nightmarish world of Ireland and Irish history. While not actually physically exiled from the geographical space known as Ireland, Banville could be said to enter into an intellectual and artistic exile, rejecting Irish concerns and dealing instead with European ones. His science tetralogy, and especially the first two novels in that series *Doctor Copernicus* (1976) and *Kepler* (1981), for instance, would seem to spearhead such a stratagem on his part, in-contestably dealing with non-Irish characters and themes. For all that, though, they do deal with history and how it is

perceived in the present. As Banville pointed out in an interview from that period:

> Since I've started writing novels based in historical
> fact I've realised that the past does not exist in terms
> of fact. It only exists in terms of the way we look at
> it, in the way that historians have looked at it. (Shee-
> han, 1979: 84)

This is a deceptively simple idea, but it has profound reso-
nances for reading and understanding history in an Irish context. Banville realises not only that the struggles about the
past are present-centred, but that the site of this struggle is
found in "writing".

In other words, history is a "fiction"; that is to say, it is a
narrative like any other narrative, and should therefore be
bound by those rules. This is not a declaration, though, that
Banville believes "history" does not matter, that the past
loses value when thought of as a fiction or that "things/
events" did not happen. Rather, he is interested in how the
past is mediated to us in the present through writing — be it
"history" writing or fictional writing. Indeed, he challenges
the usually privileged position of history writing in any cultural or national discourse by dismantling the rigid hierarchical divide between history writing and creative/artistic writing. Declan Kiberd quotes Banville slyly parodying the romantic poet Shelley by claiming that "novelists are the unac-
knowledged historians of the world" (Kiberd, 1995: 635).
Historians fail to concede how their work might be fictive,
and how novelists and novels fundamentally connect with
"history" and, thus, fail to recognise the possibility and the
necessity of productively re-imagining history.

Two of John Banville's novels in particular register the
anxieties and uncertainties surrounding the issue of the Irish
past directly: *Birchwood* (1973) and *The Newton Letter* (1982).

Birchwood is a quirky, at times chaotic, book. Like his previous novel, *Nightspawn* (1971), it is driven by a desire on the part of the author to experiment with the form of the novel, to stretch it to the very limits of credence and believability. While *Nightspawn* plays with the conventions of the thriller genre with a heady mix of spies, mystery and political intrigue on a Greek island, *Birchwood* subverts the conventions of the Anglo-Irish Big House novel tradition. There is no attempt made in either novel to be at all realistic; rather, stock characters and stereotypical plots afford the young novelist plenty of scope to play with form and meditate on his chosen themes of identity and the construction of narrative. Both novels have at their centre male narrators who are consciously and unconsciously artist figures. Each attempts to tell, or write, their story, to put some shape and order on the events of their lives in order to understand themselves and their place in the world. It is a figure that never leaves Banville's fiction.

Nightspawn has been deemed a failure by Banville himself for its clumsiness, as he says, and its "false intellectual bravado" (Imhof, 1981: 5–6). These same criticisms could be made also of *Birchwood*. For it too is clumsy and awkward in its execution, with everything in the novel appearing somewhat off-centre and a little out of place. There is, in addition, a pervasive "cleverness" to what Banville is doing that some readers might find off-putting. It is a charge that has stuck to Banville's work to the present day. However, in his defence, it can be argued that the clunky and, at times, obvious experimentation of these early novels has given way to a more confident and assured style in his later work, allowing the author to both entertain readers in a more traditional manner while still keeping faith with his intention to deal with more metaphysical concerns.

However, *Birchwood* is more successful, and indeed more interesting, than *Nightspawn*, because of its consciously Irish subject matter and themes. It operates, as has been pointed out, within the genre of the Anglo-Irish Big House novel, made famous by writers such as Maria Edgeworth in the early nineteenth century, Elizabeth Bowen and Edith Somerville and Martin Ross in the twentieth century. It is a curious feature of Banville's Irish work that he returns repeatedly to the staples of this type of fiction. Recently, he has made use of his familiarity with the tropes and images of Big House life in writing the screenplay for a cinematic version of Elizabeth Bowen's *The Last September*.

On an initial reading, *Birchwood* appears conventional enough. The first part of the novel, "The Book of the Dead", begins with Gabriel Godkin declaring that, by writing the story of his life, he can attempt to come to some understanding of that life and his present condition. The story he tells is one of family intrigue with gothic overtones, concerning the property of Birchwood Estate and its inheritance. As with all literary Anglo-Irish Big Houses, it is from the outset set on a trajectory of steady decline. Much is made of alliances and misalliances as the estate changes hands between the Lawlesses and the Godkins. His own position in the family seems secure enough until the arrival of Aunt Martha and her illegitimate son Michael. Dark hints are also made about the possibility of Gabriel having a twin sister. As Banville himself said about *Birchwood*:

> [It] has all the stereotypes: the dark, angry father; the long-suffering mother; ghastly grand-parents; the artistic son; the wild son; the strange aunt; it has them all. (Sheehan, 1979: 83)

Moreover, as if on cue, the first part closes in flames with the burning of the Big House. As the embers cool on Gabriel's home, he runs away, leaving the ruined Birchwood dwindling behind him. Many puzzles remain unresolved: "Why had Aunt Martha died? . . . Where was Michael? And my sister? All these questions, and many more. I longed for answers" (*BW*, 99).

The second part of the novel, "Air and Angels", the reader would anticipate, should offer solutions to these questions by bringing light to the dark goings-on hinted at and obliquely alluded to in the first section. Naturally, this is exactly what does not happen. Of all things, Gabriel Godkin joins a circus and so the expected progress of the narrative is seriously disrupted.

Despite the break with the Big House narrative, it can be argued that the second section is a retelling of the first part. Unquestionably, intimations of the earlier story are evident. Confusion is still to the fore. Whereas before, Gabriel was uncertain about his own family's relationship to one another, he is now perplexed with the exact nature of the connections between the various members of Prospero's circus. Although Angel appears to be the ringmaster Silas's wife, it is Sybil who is the mother to his children, the twins Justin and Juliette: "androgynous, identical, exquisite" (*BW*, 104). There is yet another set of twins, Ada and Ida, thus copper-fastening the motif set up in the first section. And then there is Prospero, whose name, borrowed from Shakespeare's *The Tempest*, invokes the idea of authorial creativity, who never appears.

In Gabriel's story, all things appear to have an opposite. Each person requires an opposite — a double or twin — to be compared against. The house of Birchwood, for instance, like all literary Big Houses, stands in opposition to the wild countryside that surrounds it, being defined by not being of the countryside. Yet, these opposites are reversed and melt into one another, and disappear, as the narrative progresses. If the world outside the Big House seems chaotic in the second part, this is but an amplification of the madness within the estate depicted in the first section of the novel. What at first seems different is found to be frighteningly identical.

The journey undertaken by Gabriel is a circular one, ending up back where he began in his home of Birchwood. His quest for his twin sister fails because there never was a twin sister in the first place. His adventures have taken him through a chaotic Ireland beset by famine and rebellion. This disintegration of the country at large mirrors the disintegration of his family and his home in the first part of the novel. His quest, in the end, throws up more questions than answers, more confusion than resolution.

The final section of the book, "Mercury", ties up all the loose ends. It is an improbable conclusion. Michael is in fact his twin brother, both of them products of an incestuous union between his father and his Aunt Martha. The quest for his sister was an illusion, perhaps a means for him to distance himself from the awful truth of his situation or simply, as Gabriel declares: "A waking, necessary fantasy. Necessary, yes . . . The future must have a locus! If not, what was the point?" (*BW*, 138). The narrative ends with Gabriel ruminating on his newly found knowledge and his position as a writer attempting to come to some sort of understanding about the story he has just told and the people he has known:

> I began to write, as a means of finding them again, and thought that at last I had discovered a form which would contain and order all my losses. I was wrong. There is no form, no order, only echoes and coincidences, sleight of hand, dark laughter. I accept it. (*BW*, 174)

The note of failure struck so eloquently here brings this particular work to an end, but it reverberates also throughout Banville's entire subsequent fictional output.

What, then, is the reader to make of this work? The expected elements of the traditional ascendancy Big House novel are certainly paid due homage. Of course, it is thoroughly exaggerated, resulting in an almost cartoonish quality

to the events and the characters in that everything that does
happen should happen and everybody that should be there is
indeed there. Just as the reader could be said to be coming
to grips with this playful parody, the narrative moves from
the relative stability of the Big House into an archetypal tale
of "running away to join the circus". This is disconcerting
and is meant to be. Banville recalls his American publisher
being aghast at this turn of events and recommending that
he discard the entire second part (Sheehan, 1979: 84). One
purpose, perhaps, in making his character leave the confines
of the Big House is that Banville can register that there is life
beyond its walls. By mingling two separate genres in this
way, he highlights that one form, or genre or discourse, can
never fully encompass Ireland as an idea or a story.

Rüdiger Imhof adjudges the contrivances of *Birchwood* —
the set of readymade themes and stereotypical plots and
characters — to be proof that it is not a Big House novel as
such, but rather a convenient backdrop for him to exploit
for his playfully postmodernist purposes (Imhof, 1997: 57). In
this reading, the focus shifts from the outward bric-a-brac of
ascendancy life and Big House decline, inward to the story-
telling consciousness of Gabriel Godkin and the fiction he
creates. Elements within the story, the numerous sets of
twins for example, are brought to the fore as postmodern
signs of rupture and incompleteness: twins and twinning being a manifestation of the divided self and the breakdown of
the enlightenment ideal of a coherent single identity. They
are an indication too of Gabriel's fractured consciousness
and suggest the difficulties at the heart of his narrative.

He is in search of a narrative of order and harmony
which will transfigure his world of disconnected fragments. It
will, hopefully, be a story that can place everything in connection with everything else. In the first section of the novel,
there is a scene when Michael begins to juggle:

> At first it went clumsily, he dropped the ball, hit
> himself on the nose with the block, but then all
> abruptly, a rhythm appeared, one could almost hear
> it, like the airy beat of a bird's wing, and in his hands
> he spun a trembling pale blue hoop of light . . . I
> found myself thinking of air and angels, of silence, of
> translucent planes of pale blue glass in space gliding
> through illusory, gleaming and perfect combinations.
> (BW, 43)

His own toy, his jigsaw puzzle, is described as "a paltry
thing" in comparison to this "beauty, this, this harmony"
(BW, 43). Even the awed stuttering here denotes the goal of
Gabriel's narrative labours: perfection. Yet Gabriel recognises that the harmony and beauty displayed here are only
momentary and fleeting. Juggling can be seen as an anticipa-
tion of the circus motif in the second section of the novel.
Thus, the magic of the circus, its make-believe improvisa-
tions and ramshackle coherence only truly coming together
in performance, becomes a means of understanding art and
the act of writing. Writing is an endeavour to create moments of beauty and order amid the chaos of its own creation. As Gabriel says: "Violets and cowshit; my life has been
ever thus" (BW, 132).

It is a feature of Banville's writing that he is able to recreate wonderful scenes that have the ability to stand apart
and alone from the rest of the narrative. This novel is no
different. Gabriel's mad grandfather, for instance, discovered
in death in the birch wood with his false teeth sunk into the
bark of a tree; the scene of his grandmother's death by
spontaneous combustion; or the moment that he realises
that moments are all that we can know:

> Each time I blinked I carried back from the gloom an
> image of arrested movement, the old man frozen in
> mid-air, Silas with his arm uplifted, the fat woman

> with a finger stuck in her red eye, and it came to me
> with the clarity and beauty of a mathematical state-
> ment that all movement is composed of an infinity of
> minute stillnesses . . . It was enormously pleasing,
> this discovery of fixity within continuity . . . And I
> saw . . . that this was how I lived, glancing every now
> and then out of the darkness and catching sly time in
> the act, but such glimpses were rare and brief and of
> hardly any consequence, for time, time would go on
> anyway, without my vigilance. (BW, 128)

Illuminated glimpses of the world are numerous and varied,
the problem being to bring them together, to make them
mean something:

> Such scenes as this I see, or imagine I see, no differ-
> ence, through a glass sharply. The light is lucid,
> steady, and does not glance in spikes or starts from
> bright things, but shines in cool cubes, planes and
> violet lines and lines within planes, as light trapped in
> polished crystal shine. Indeed, now that I think of it, I
> feel it is not a glass through which I see, but rather a
> gathering of perfect prisms . . . Outside my memo-
> ries, this silence and harmony, this brilliance I find
> again in that second silent world which exists, inde-
> pendent, ordered by unknown laws, in the depths of
> mirrors. This is how I remember such scenes. If I
> provide something otherwise, be assured I am in-
> venting. (BW, 21)

Nevertheless, invention is what holds these separate scenes
together: it is the glue that binds them. Yet, as the imagery
used — of prisms and mirrors — makes clear, this invention
cannot truly connect with the real world, which is always
maddeningly just beyond reach, just escaping expression.

In consequence, it can be argued that what is of importance in *Birchwood* is not so much the story being told —

because in truth, it cannot be told adequately — but the act of telling itself. Gabriel's personal and individual history and his sense of self are what are at stake in the novel and the wider concerns of Irish history are to be ignored. Rüdiger Imhof makes much of a blurb on an early edition of *Birchwood*. The blurb reads that this is Banville's "brilliant novel of Ireland in chaos". Of course, Imhof argues that this is exactly what the novel cannot be, owing to the fact that it focuses on the individual predicament of Gabriel Godkin (Imhof, 1998: 57). By concentrating wholly on Gabriel's individual plight, a general sense of history is negated in that the understanding he comes to at the close of the novel — that all is fiction — is a singular glimpse of truth rather than a collective truth:

> We imagine that we remember things as they were,
> while in fact all we carry into the future are fragments
> which reconstruct a wholly illusory past (*BW*, 12).

Indeed, it is a truth that stresses the primacy of the individual. His admission that there never is a Prospero, that he has "become his own Prospero" (*BW* 172) and, in turn, ours, suggests that each of us necessarily invents his or her own individual story. The almost moral imperative, then, is to create oneself because that is all that is possible: nobody else can tell that story and, obviously, it is impossible to tell other people's stories.

James Joyce felt that the position of the artist in relation to his art should be one of being God-like, of being "indifferent, paring his fingernails" (Joyce, 1984: 194). Banville might be mischievously playing with this aesthetic by naming his narrator Gabriel Godkin. In *Birchwood*, the reader discovers that Gabriel is not nonchalantly god-like in terms of the story he tells or the authority he wields, nor is he, like his namesake the archangel, a messenger to be wholly trusted.[1] Can the same be said of John Banville, the author of *Birchwood*?

Our reading of *Birchwood* thus far is dependent on one crucial factor: that John Banville, as author, is master of the narrative he creates. It is one of the paradoxes at the heart of postmodern writing that, while it displays or enacts chaos, randomness, chance, and indeterminacy, it is still a highly worked — or wrought — art form. It is as if postmodern writers are capable of "talking about" the breakdown of old narratives and systems of thought, of the impossibility of writing itself, but they, themselves, do not succumb fully to the conclusions that their writing necessarily leads to. In *Birchwood*, for instance, Banville tells of how he intentionally set out to confound his reader's expectations. The unevenness of the plot and the jarring quality of the narrative breaks and skips are all conscious on the part of the author: he is very much in control of his novel (Sheehan, 1979: 82). So much so that, in fact, his toil and labour as an author are not hidden and invisible as Joyce's dictum stipulates. As a postmodern writer, Banville is aware of the aspirational nature of such an aesthetic, realising that detachment of this quality is merely an illusion. Indeed, writing like Banville's sets out to explode this illusion by blatantly displaying the fictive nature of what is being presented. Thus, his authorial fingerprints are to be discovered throughout the text. There is even a moment when Banville appears, however furtively, in the novel itself. When Gabriel is travelling with the circus, he must take part in the troupe's act in order to earn his keep. He has no skills like the others and merely does a turn as the comic foil in Silas's magic act. He pretends to be a

---

[1] There is, though, a more mundane reading of the name "Godkin": that it is a real family name. Thus, even when he would appear to be most playfully postmodern, Banville is in fact only reflecting an Irish reality.

member of the audience who volunteers to be hypnotised and the name he offers is "Johann Livelb", an anagram of "John Banville". It is a ruse he uses again in his later novel *Athena* where the numerous paintings described in the text are created by various versions of "John Banville". With regard to *Birchwood*, it means that Gabriel and Banville become one, albeit only for an instant.

Thus, Gabriel's problems with discovering a form or a language that can contain and tell his story can be said to be John Banville's problems too — though presented at one remove. While all of Banville's main critics are in agreement with this reading of his work and its self-referential nature, most are unable to explore fully the implications of transferring Gabriel's anxieties to the author Banville. Doing so can alter our reading and understanding of this work, transforming the personal tragedy of Gabriel Godkin into a tragedy of wider, national, proportions, revolving round the nature and status of Irish history in the contemporary moment.

Banville's use of the Big House genre is not simply one of convenience. History has been intrinsically linked to the Big House novel from its inception. The best of these novels, since Maria Edgeworth's *Castle Rackrent*, published on the eve of the implementation of the Act of Union of Great Britain and Ireland in 1800, have opened up a space for both the writer and the reader to explore the relationship between fiction and history. Novels such as Elizabeth Bowen's *The Last September* (1929), set during the Anglo-Irish War of Independence of 1919–1921, or George Moore's *A Drama in Muslin* (1886), set during the land wars of the 1880s, register the turbulence and shifts of, and in, Irish history (Kreilkamp, 1998: 1–25). Indeed, the Irish Big House novel is best suited to considering these tensions, as it brings together Irish and English, Protestant and Catholic, landlord and peasant under the one roof where their respective identities and myths can be questioned and probed.

Birchwood's historical backdrop cannot be confined to one single moment or event. The framework to Gabriel's personal story is, as we know, an Ireland of famine and rebellion. The decline of the Godkins in the first section of the novel, "The Book of the Dead", on one level reflects the financial and economic descent of the Anglo-Irish brought about by the Land Acts of the late nineteenth and early twentieth centuries. However, closer inspection of the text reveals a very fluid sense of Ireland's past. Various rebellions from different times, including the War of Independence, along with a reference to an early nineteenth-century revolutionary group, the Molly Maguires, are all seen to be occurring simultaneously in the novel. There are allusions also to the agrarian unrest of the nineteenth century and to the great famine of the 1840s. Telephones and bicycles appear at times when they should not, if Banville were being faithful to the facts of the past.

To read *Birchwood* simply as a postmodern pastiche and parody of the Big House novel would suggest that, for Banville, Irish history is no longer a nightmare. That he is able to manipulate his material, play with these allusions to many of the major events of Ireland's history of the last two hundred years, could be understood as a signal that history is over and done with and thus available for such a playfully postmodern treatment. However, it is not simply a case that Banville repudiates Irish history or places himself in an ironic position to Ireland's past, though some of his critics would wish that this were so.

In a 1992 TV interview with the broadcaster David Hanly, Banville with regard to *Birchwood*, acknowledged that in retrospect he "discovered how much of Ireland there was in it, how much of the early seventies there was in it. When Northern Ireland was beginning to be really bad" (RTE, 1992). It is a curious admission on the part of the author. It suggests, at some level, a loss of control over his narrative.

The terrible violence of that time ruptures a sense of Irish history as being "done" and "finished", of its being of the past. The boundary between the past and the present become blurred, resulting in a chaotic "nightmare". It is a "nightmare" precisely because of this chronological indeterminacy. There is a moment in the novel when "contemporary" violence, it could be argued, enters the text in the voice of an English soldier who declares "micks" to be "barmy!" (*BW*, 146). The language and tone appear utterly "modern" and out of place, even in this most chaotic of texts.

The problem in *Birchwood*, then, is one of representation and the inability to find an adequate form that will contain and fix Ireland's history. The past cannot be put into perspective: a whole, complete picture of the past cannot be obtained in the present and thus only disorderly fragments can be offered. Banville's position here echoes that of Gabriel, who can only manage to offer moments of harmony and beauty while the whole remains just out of reach.

Irish history, then, cannot be so easily "escaped" as some might hope; it is still problematic in the present day. It is interesting that Banville singles out the problem of the North of Ireland. It is as if he were acknowledging that, owing to this situation, the past could not be left behind because, in a very real way, progress and development had not been allowed to happen — that the "past" is not yet safely over and done with. The situation in the North means that history continues to be a nightmare in the contemporary Irish situation.

There are a number of conclusions about the nature of history to be drawn from *Birchwood*. In terms of reading history, the implication is that, in the present, the debate should not be about what happened factually but rather about the reading of history as a comment on who is writing it and why. In her study, *The Feminization of Famine*,[2] Margaret Kelleher considers how famine has been represented in Irish literature in the nineteenth and twentieth centuries. She suggests that the use of women to "express" the horrors of famine was a means for certain writers contemporary to the disaster to conceal the political and economic causes that produce famine. Similarly, Banville wants us to attend to the various "echoes and coincidences, sleights of hand" that go into making "history".

By presenting "history" as "fiction", by dismantling the hierarchical opposition between fact and myth, Banville demonstrates how historical and mythological narratives are made. Moreover, it allows him to move beyond a deadening narrative "determinism" toward a fictional space of radical indeterminacy. Indeed, in a general way, due to this postmodernist "playing" with history, it could be said that he escapes the tyranny of logic and coherence, and is thus free to create significance on his own terms and by his own means. At one point, Gabriel declares that "the present is unthinkable" (*BW*, 138), and that all that is available to his imagination is his past and his future. It is the past upon which his creative imagination dwells most, but it is through this engagement with the past that a future might be made possible. So too with Banville's engagement with Irish history: he hopes to "open" history up to new readings and interpretations, unlocking the past in order to free himself into a more productive encounter with the future.

The final lines of Gabriel Godkin's narrative proclaim: "whereof I cannot speak, thereof I must be silent" (*BW*, 175). This phrase, a direct quotation from the philosopher

---

[2] Margaret Kelleher (1997), *The Feminization of Famine: Expressions of the Inexpressible?* Cork: Cork University Press. Significantly, Kelleher focuses on Banville's *Birchwood* because of the manner in which it self-consciously deals with its own act of "telling".

Ludwig Wittgenstein, acknowledges that the limits of one's language are the limits of one's world, with each individual trapped within his or her own world. However silence is not of this world, Banville and his narrators are condemned to break that silence by speaking, by creating stories that endeavour to map their, and our, experience.

This is, at once, both a liberating position and a form of imprisonment. It is liberating because, quite simply, any future becomes possible. Near the end of his narrative, Gabriel says:

> Outside is destruction and decay. I do not speak the language of this wild country. I will stay here, alone, and live a life different from any the house has ever known. Yes. (*BW*, 174)

Hope remains that a new language, a new form, might yet potentially say what has not been said. Only by returning again and again to the past can such a future come to pass. But a nightmarish situation still exists: writing offers a means of dealing with the past and history but it also acknowledges that all attempts at such understanding through acts of writing will necessarily fail.

Undoubtedly, *Birchwood* is a parody, a pastiche made up of numerous bits and pieces of various Big House novels. But it is unfair to think of this background as a comic *tour de force*, allowing the author to ruminate on his chosen themes concerning memory and imagination in the foreground. His depiction of the ravages of Irish war and famine signify the utter seriousness at the heart of this fictional enterprise. There is real emotion to the tragedy being played out in this novel, captured in those fleeting moments when the narrator Gabriel's sense of wonder is charged by the mystery of the world and transcendent understanding seems possible and, indeed, communicable. That these moments are shot through with the knowledge that Banville and his character's attempts to discover order and meaning are useless, does not undermine them completely. It is the paradox of a postmodern existence that is being expressed here; a balancing act between hope and despair, between utterance and silence. Happily, Banville chooses to continue to write and in doing so, forces his readers to look again at what they thought they already knew.

Following *Birchwood*, John Banville embarked on what has become known as his science tetralogy. It was an ambitious project of four novels intending to deal with the lives of four European scientists, Nicholas Copernicus, Johannes Kepler, Isaac Newton and Albert Einstein. Only the first two novels in this series, *Doctor Copernicus* (1976) and *Kepler* (1981), held to this initial blueprint. While not dealing with observably Irish themes, these two works do clearly demonstrate his deepening interest in the nature of history and its relevance to the contemporary moment, while also furthering his examination of the creative imagination. However, the last two novels of the series, *The Newton Letter: An Interlude* (1982) and *Mefisto* (1986), return Banville's fiction to an Irish environment.

The Newton Letter, in a way, begins where *Birchwood* left off nearly ten years previously. If *Birchwood* suggested that our knowledge of the past is accessible only through texts, that there is no other means of connecting with the past, then this is precisely the predicament that faces the main character in *The Newton Letter*. In a sense, he must deal with the ramifications of Gabriel Godkin's hard-won knowledge.

After the overtly historical structure of his previous fictions, Banville sets this novel in the contemporary moment. It is not, though, an abandonment of the past, since it is the past by profession and by inclination that the narrator of *The Newton Letter* — a historian — wishes so desperately to understand. Writing a critical biography of the scientist Isaac Newton, he returns home to Ireland and Wexford to complete the project. He rents the gate lodge of Fern House, seeking peace and quiet, installing himself comfortably for the hard work ahead, of recreating the great scientist's life. Things, naturally, do not go according to plan. The historian's own estimation of events are brusque and to the point:

> I spent a summer in the country, I slept with one woman and thought I was in love with another; I dreamed up a horrid drama, and failed to the see the commonplace tragedy that was playing itself out in real life. (*NL,* 79)

While this, indeed, is a fair outline of the plot, it belies the intricacies and brilliance of the fiction Banville presents his readers. This is one of his shorter works and is, in truth, a novella rather than a fully extended piece of writing. Nonetheless, Banville manages to compress a great deal into the compact space he allows himself. The pressure of scope, it could be argued, forces from Banville a consummate performance where every word, every sentence, connects with the totality of the novel's intention. While *Birchwood* did possess a certain intimacy, in that the focus was on a single character, in *The Newton Letter* this is even more so the case. The wider concerns of Irish history as presented in *Birchwood* are here telescoped and presented on the micro level. It is, or as near as it is possible to be, quite perfect and perhaps his best piece of writing.

A tetralogy in Greek literature was a series of four dramas: three tragedies and one satire. In Banville's science series *Doctor Copernicus, Kepler,* and *Mefisto* are the tragic parts, while *The Newton Letter,* as its subtitle "An Interlude" intimates, corresponds to the satiric piece of the tetralogy. Rüdiger Imhof claims he is unable to ascertain where exactly the satire "really resides in the book" (Imhof, 1997: 238). He is unable to do so because of his persistent disregard for considering Banville as having anything to say about the Irish condition. The satire within the novel is directed toward Banville himself as a writer writing fictions in Ireland. For Banville — like his historian completing a biography on Isaac Newton — had been, in his previous two novels, writing about real historical characters, and in this novel he now questions that activity, exploring and examining the nature of his own acts of writing. Thus, the historian's problems, at some level, reflect Banville's own predicament with the past and the ways in which it is mediated to us in the present.

Banville has stated that one of the informing sources for *The Newton Letter* is Henry James's novel *The Europeans*. At the heart of James's novel is a variation of the theme he deals with in works like *Portrait of a Lady* and *The Aspern Papers*: the collision of the New World of America with the Old World of European values and thought. In *The Europeans*, this is reversed in that the movement is from the old to the new. Central to these novels is a "cultural clash" based on the misconceptions and misunderstandings that each group has of the other. Imhof, again unsurprisingly, declares an inability to make any connection between James's novel and Banville's (Imhof, 1997: 144). It is crucial, though, to register the corresponding nature of the pivotal "cultural clash" upon which *The Newton Letter* revolves.

Upon arriving at Fern House, the historian declares that:

> I had them spotted for patricians from the start. The big house, Edward's tweeds, Charlotte's fine-boned slender grace that the dowdiest of clothes could not mask, even Ottilie's awkwardness, all this seemed the unmistakable stamp of their class. Protestants, of course, landed, the land now gone to gombeen men and compulsory purchase, the family fortune wasted by tax, death duties, inflation. (*NL*, 12)

It is well-known territory for Banville's readers: the Big House inhabited by a cast of familiar Anglo-Irish characters. What is markedly different from *Birchwood* is that the narrator is, as he says himself, the "product of a post-peasant Catholic upbringing" (*NL*, 12). This adds a certain tension to the narrative, absent in the earlier novel. Gabriel Godkin had declared that he did not "speak the language of this wild country" (*BW*, 174), thus locking himself into a purely Anglo-Irish discourse. Here, the reader is presented with a narrator from outside the Big House demesne looking in, a character who is of that "wild country" and does indeed speak its language.

There is a collision, then, of cultures: Irish is set against Anglo-Irish. It is a broadening of Banville's engagement with Irish themes and issues, allowing him the opportunity to not only demonstrate yet again how history or the past is written and created in the present, but to test also how these versions of the past operate in the present contemporary moment. Whereas the act of writing was the focus in *Birchwood*, the act of reading now comes to the fore in *The Newton Letter*. Or, perhaps, misreading would be more appropriate.

This is a story about misconceptions and misinterpretations, a sort of social comedy based on expectations being consistently undermined. As one would anticipate with an "Interlude", the emphasis in this novel is mostly light-hearted. But, as is the case with all of Banville's novels, dark humour and black comedy serve only to heighten the tragedy of his characters' predicaments.

In *Birchwood*, Gabriel at one point says, "all thinking is in a sense remembering" (*BW*, 11). The reverse is also shown to be true: that memory itself is a necessarily creative act. Similarly, in *The Newton Letter*, reading becomes an imaginative exercise for the narrator. As a historian, our expectations are that he will deal with facts, that his act of reading will be an objectively critical one. However, the historian is, basically, a closet novelist, much more interested in the romantic possibilities of his surroundings as coloured by the numerous literary works he has read.

Little clues are scattered throughout the narrative as to the type of fiction the historian enjoys. When he sees Fern House for the first time, he describes it as being a "big gloomy pile with ivy and peeling walls and a smashed fanlight over the door, the kind of place where you picture a mad step-daughter locked up in the attic" (*NL*, 3). Charlotte Brontë's nineteenth-century novel *Jane Eyre* and her character Bertha Mason are being comically alluded to here. His early observations of the Lawless family (the name, of course, should be familiar to readers of *Birchwood*) going about their morning business conjure up the mood of a "pastoral mime, with the shepherd's wife and the shepherd, and Cupid and the maid" (*NL*, 12) This is a gentle nod to the seventeenth-century writer Andrew Marvell and his pastoral poetry, especially his "Mower" poems with their "pastures, caves and springs" (Marvell, 1967: 61). There are many other echoes of numerous literary works from James Joyce and Henry James to John Milton's *Paradise Lost*.

It must be noted that such weaving of direct quotations and more subtle, ethereal reference to other works of writing is a constant feature of Banville's fiction. In an interview, he explained clearly his reasoning behind this stratagem:

> We're part of a tradition, a European tradition; why not acknowledge it. And then, books are to a large extent made out of other books; why not acknowledge that too. Also, I find the incorporation of references to other works, and even quotations from these works, give the text a peculiar and interesting resonance, which is registered even when the reader does not realise that something is being quoted. (Imhof, 1987: 13)

The postmodern world is one made up of texts, and texts produce only more texts, and are constructed out of past texts. A book like *The Newton Letter*, for instance, becomes a

repository of past writing and knowledge, as indeed was
Birchwood, where quotations from Descartes and Wittgenstein open and close the novel. While Banville, the author,
seems to be in control of his literary allusions, consciously
inserting them in order to produce certain impressions in
his readership, the same cannot be said of the narrator. The
difficulty for the historian is that his predisposition to perceive the world in literary terms means that reality and immediate experience become obscured.

He has, as we know, identified the Lawless family as
members of the Anglo-Irish Protestant ascendancy from his
first encounters with them. Every nuance and detail copper-
fastens this early impression of the family:

> The form their refinement took was wholly familiar
> to me: wellington boots, henhouses, lumpy sweaters.
> Familiar, but, oh, transfigured. . . . Their ordinariness
> was inimitable. (*NL*, 13)

His imagination is hungry for more evidence of their aristocratic bearing. They attend "church" rather than "Mass",
returning to a light lunch instead of the post-peasant Catholic fare of the "mighty roast . . . steeped marrowfat peas,
[and a] block of runny ice-cream" (*NL*, 13). Each culture
possesses its own code with an appropriate language and
pool of accessible imagery.

Every character has their prescribed role to play in this
Big House fiction based on past Big House fictions. Edward
has the unenviable part of the sot: "I saw the whole thing
now, of course: he was a waster" (*NL*, 19). Charlotte, his
wife, is the aloof matriarch who is mostly silent or "perhaps
hard of hearing. The possibility was oddly touching" (*NL*, 14).
Ottilie, their niece, is many things, and the narrator's physical affair with her, that intimate contact, seems to lessen his
ability to create a suitable role for her in his imagined Big
House world. Yet her idea of her parents as a "kind of Scott

and Zelda, beautiful and doomed, hair blown back and white silk scarves whipping in the wind as they sailed blithely, laughing, down the slipstream of disaster" (*NL*, 28), conjures up Scott Fitzgerald's description of wealthy people from his *The Great Gatsby*:

> They were careless people . . . they smashed up things and creatures and then retreated back into their money or their vast carelessness, or whatever it was that kept them together, and let other people clean up the mess they had made. (Scott Fitzgerald, 1984: 186)

Even Ottilie is marked out as the product of a landed gentry at once destructively careless but fascinating to behold: the beautiful and the damned indeed.

One particular Irish literary figure from the past haunts the pages of *The Newton Letter*. A variety of echoes and allusions to the Big House poetry of W.B. Yeats are scattered throughout the novella. There is a chestnut tree in the yard, a "great rooted blossomer" (*NL*, 19), making a direct link to Yeats's "Among School Children":

> O chestnut tree, great-rooted blossomer,
> Are you the leaf, the blossom or the bole?
> O body swayed to music, O brightening glance,
> How can we know the dancer from the dance?
>   (Yeats, 1985: 245)

For Yeats, the tree was a symbol of Anglo-Irish rootedness and tradition and, therefore, it is wholly proper that the Lawlesses should possess such a tree and that above the demesne wood a hawk — another of the poet's aristocratic images — should be hunting. Charlotte, the historian's beloved, is in turn an image of refined Yeatsian womanhood:

> I stopped to look at her, the dark glossy head, the
> pale neck . . . light of evening, the tall windows —
> oh, a gazelle! (*NL*, 40)

The imagery here recalls Yeats's poem "In Memory of Eva
Gore-Booth and Countess Markiewicz":

> The light of evening, Lissadell,
> Great windows open to the south,
> Two girls in silk kimonos, both
> Beautiful, one a gazelle. (Yeats, 1985: 263)

Though there is certainly a playfulness to Banville's visualisa-
tion of a Yeatsian aristocracy — at one stage Edward un-
ceremoniously urinates against the trunk of the great chestnut tree (*NL*, 33) — it serves also to connect the historian
with the Yeatsian position of being outside the Big House
and desperately desiring to be on the inside. Though Yeats
was an Anglo-Irish Protestant, he was not of the same class
or status as his friend and literary colleague Lady Gregory,
for instance. In other words, an awed reverence for the
style of Big House life unites our narrator with the poet.

Crucial, too, is that Yeats's poetic enterprise is an act of
mythologising the Anglo-Irish. So effective is this process of
literary veneration, that his myth of history becomes myth
as history. And our narrator, who should, in truth, know
better (he is, after all, a historian), succumbs whole-
heartedly to this mythologising and is unable — and, perhaps, unwilling — to see beyond his programmed expectations of what Big House living should be like, to the reality
of the Lawlesses' existence.

The very real problem, then, that Banville is dealing with
is the propensity in the Irish situation to deal with various
versions of history as fact — be it nationalist, colonial, un-
ionist or revisionist history. He could also be commenting
on how in Ireland certain literary fictions — such as Yeats's

"Big House" — have a power that extends far beyond any social reality, and how these types of "myths of history" are more popular and powerful than "real" history.

Banville himself has said that *The Newton Letter* is one of his favourite pieces of work because almost every sentence contains a misconception in it and that for him this is as close to his original intention for the novella as is possible (Ní Anluain, 2000: 40). He says, too, that this is one of the main reasons why it is a comic book. Yet, despite the comedy, the tragedy at the heart of *The Newton Letter* is a real and a very human one. The historian, blinded to the actuality of the drama playing out before him and so overwhelmingly eager to read every detail of Fern House life as proof positive of his Big House reading of the situation, is entrapped in a fantasy world of his own mad creation. In *Birchwood*, Gabriel's fiction was an insular one, in that it affected only himself: his was a personal act of myth-making. Here, the historian's myth-making consciousness does impinge upon the reality out of which he creates his fantasies. There are consequences, not for only for himself, but also for those people he imagines he knows so well.

On his first journey to Fern House, the historian remarks on the trivial things he sees from his train window:

> The shy back-end of things, drainpipes and broken windows, . . . a white cloud . . . slowly cruising the horizon. What has all this to do with anything? Yet such remembered scraps seem to me abounding in significance. They are at once commonplace and unique, like the clues at the scene of a crime. But everything that day was still innocent as the blue sky itself, so what do they prove? Perhaps just that: the innocence of things, their non-complicity in our affairs. All the same I'm convinced those drainpipes and that cloud require me far more desperately that I do them. (*NL*, 1–2)

Banville's description here of the "shy back-end of things" can be read as a kind of aesthetic manifesto for his entire fictional output. It is a wonderful expression of the dilemma of the contemporary postmodern artist: it acknowledges the rupture between the human mind and the world of nature, but also attests to the obsessive human need to engage with that reality. In terms of the historian's predicament, it implies that significance is to be discovered everywhere; and not only that, significance must be actively sought out. Later, he recalls childhood train journeys to Dublin city and once again the reader is offered an insight into the historian's motivations:

> I would gaze at that silent house and wonder, in a hunger of curiosity, what lives were lived there . . . I knew, of course, those hidden lives wouldn't be much different from my own. But that was the point. It wasn't the exotic I was after, but the ordinary, that strangest and most elusive of enigmas. (*NL*, 11)

In Joycean fashion, the historian believes that the quotidian — the everyday and the commonplace — is what is truly extraordinary. However, this is precisely what is not afforded the narrator because of his overactive desire to make his world extraordinary: the world needs him to tell its story and he will do just that. In other words, the historian discovers an almost stereotypical example of Big House life in the contemporary moment: a family teetering on financial ruin but facing that end with enviably stylish equanimity, because this is what he expects or hopes to find. Quite simply, he forces square pegs into round holes; he bends reality to the demands of his expectations.

There are, surprisingly for such a short, compact book, numerous layers to Banville's treatment of the historian and the fictions he weaves. What can be called the first layer or level of fiction-making is that fiction the historian makes, remakes, revises and adds to continually upon his arrival at Fern House. He says of the place that "It was the name that attracted me" (*NL*, 3). Readers should always attend to names in Banville's books because they can be a source of information regarding the story being told. In *Birchwood*, for instance, the name of Gabriel Godkin has repercussions for an understanding of his position in the novel: a messenger with authority, or so the reader is led to believe. The name of Lawless, common to both *Birchwood* and *The Newton Letter*, should indicate, obviously, a sense of turbulence and possible upheaval of the predictable pattern of the traditional novel form. So it is with the name of Fern House. A fern is a vascular cryptogam, a plant which possesses no stamens or pistils and therefore has no flowers or seeds (no organs of reproduction). Cryptogam stems from "crypto" meaning something concealed or secret, which comes from the Greek word "krupto" meaning hidden; and "gamos" which is Greek for marriage. Thus Fern House is transformed into a place of secrets, hidden meanings and connections; a place well suited to an imagination that hopes to lay bare the mysteries of everyday objects. And mystery is to be discovered everywhere and in everything.

The inhabitants of Fern House are riddlesome. Despite their fitting into a preordained Big House pattern, many questions remain: what exactly is the relationship between Edward and Charlotte: husband and wife or brother and sister? And who is the father of the boy Michael? Even the very grounds surrounding Fern House themselves appear to have secrets, or certainly, a self-possession that produces a corresponding disquiet in the historian — paths led him, as he says, "surreptitiously" astray (*NL*, 16).

The historian's work on Newton is very much secondary for most of the novel, or would seem to be so. Though, as Banville presents this story, the fate of the great scientist is linked to the fate of the historian, but this only becomes clear in the latter sections of the work. Suffice it to say that early on, the historian's interest in the book wanes and his interest in the Big House and its inhabitants gains momentum. Not only is he convinced of his interpretation of their lives; he wants to place himself at the centre of his creation. As a "post-peasant" Catholic, their style and grace under pressure remain eminently attractive to him, and yet he never cedes complete authority to that image. His fixing of his image of them is an act of assertion, a power play between versions of history, with him very much in a position of control.

It could be argued that his fawning attitude is ultimately patronising rather than celebratory. His vision of the Anglo-Irish, in steady and terminal decline from better days, is a stereotypical image of the Anglo-Irish politically and financially neutered in post-independence Ireland. Irish novelist and critic Seamus Deane has declared that the continued presence of the Anglo-Irish Big House novel in Irish writing highlights the narrowness and poverty of that tradition as a whole (Deane, 1985: 32). Yet, Banville's bewitched and bothered historian could, unconsciously, represent a general trend in the Irish psyche: an interest in a certain image of the Anglo-Irish, one where they no longer exercise power of any kind, their very declension proof of the new ascendancy in Irish life and culture.

That imaginative power and assertiveness are at the heart of the historian's fiction can be in no doubt. He begins an affair with Ottilie, though ironically this physical contact checks his imaginative interest in her: "from the first I had assumed that I understood her absolutely, so there was no need to speculate much about her" (*NL*, 53). In other words, he dismisses her importance in relation to his desire to be at the centre of his Big House fantasy. He finds that his fiction becomes complete when he realises that he has fallen in love with the older woman, Charlotte. As he lies on his bed, he

waits for his world to readjust itself to this new element in
his design:

> The secret pattern of the past months was now re-
> vealed . . . I was like an artist blissfully checking over
> his plan of a work that has suddenly come to him
> complete in every detail, touching the marvellous,
> still-damp construct gently here and there with the
> soft feelers of imagination. Ottilie a sketch, on the
> oboe . . . Edward at once the comic relief and the
> shambling villain of the piece. Michael a Cupid still,
> the subtlety of whose aim, however, I had underes-
> timated. Even the unbroken fine summer weather
> was part of the plot. (*NL*, 42–3)

There is a place for everything and everything is in place;
nothing is left to chance — even the weather is included in
his creation. Banville has consistently retained that sense of
wonder about how the human consciousness works and
creates so that this type of moment is repeated again and
again in his writing, a moment when the inner workings of
the imagination are made almost palpable.

However, his problem is now one of sustaining his fiction. He feels as if he is out of time, as if his life in Fern
House was a "self-contained unit separate from the time of
the ordinary world" (*NL*, 49). The world "out there" is beyond his imaginative control, and must be kept at bay. Yet
the threat, as always in postmodern fiction of this type,
comes from within.

The zenith to his creative powers is reached when he
produces a pure fiction in the shape of "Charlottilie" which,
he claims, was "neither herself nor the other, but a third"
(*NL*, 48). The physical presence of Ottilie is fused with the
ideal Charlotte to make this Hegelian synthesis of the real
and ideal become one. The historian then goes on to ask:
"Was there . . . another Ottilie as well, an autochthonous

companion for that other I? Were all at Ferns dividing thus and multiplying, like amoebas?" (*NL*, 49).

While the notion of multiple self-hood is at the heart of modernism, the loss of the authentic self in this proliferation of selves is central to understanding the postmodern project. Perhaps he is not alone in dreaming up horrid dramas? Perhaps each person in Fern House could be creating a world around themselves? The reader may be witness to only one story of this summer spent in the countryside, but it may be simply one among a multitude of stories. For the historian who delights in his own Big House story, this is indeed a challenge.

Cracks, or rather major fissures, begin to appear in his assumptions about the Lawlesses. A casual remark from Ottilie one Sunday morning that she had skipped the family excursion to Mass in order to spend the time with him has devastating consequences for his fantasy: "Mass? They were Catholics? My entire conception of them had to be revised" (*NL*, 54).

A single word carries the weight of a whole culture. Yet, there had been numerous signals for the astute reader to decode: the presence of a hurley stick in the hall, for instance. Or when the Lawlesses are entertaining guests, a comment is made about commemorating 27 August 1979. The narrator presumes that they want to acknowledge Lord Mountbatten, killed on that day along with three others by the Provisional IRA in Mullaghmore, County Sligo: "One of their dwindling band of heroes, cruelly murdered. I was charmed: only they would dare to make a memorial of a drawing-room tea party" (*NL*, 37).

In fact, the opposite is true. The guest disabuses him of his awed admiration for steely reticence by celebrating that death and the death of 18 British soldiers at Warrenpoint on the same day. The historian, so assured of his own ability to read the signs, ignores both these emblems indicating a nationalist heritage. Another point to be made is that a moment like this belies so much of the criticism surrounding Banville's work, which argues that it is interested solely in the esoteric and the abstract. A reader might be hard put to find any more direct reference to the situation in Northern Ireland in the 1970s and 1980s.

Despite these intrusions, the historian continues on blithely with his Big House illusion of genteel life and ritual. It is only when Ottilie directly confronts the historian's version of events, telling him that, "You don't know anything. You think you are so clever, but you don't know a thing," that he begins to question his assumptions. He now feels as though he has been turned into glass, "as if the world could shine through me unimpeded: as if I were now a quicksilver shadow in someone else's looking-glass fantasy" (*NL*, 57). Here, the cultural clash upon which the novella rotates comes to the fore. This affront to the historian's author(ity) produces an unexpected and violent outburst in the historian: he slaps her hard across the face. Challenged with the idea that he may not be right, that what he has held as true is a fiction, he cannot express his indignation. He is unable to find the word or words that will silence this humiliation, fictionalise it and make it part of his creation and thus this loss of control, this absence, is filled with this very real and powerful moment of violence. So, behind the light-hearted emphasis on social comedy based on a series of misconceptions and misreadings, lurks a violent reality. Indeed, in a specifically Irish situation, the importance of narrative is accentuated: stories, or culture in general, become a way to contain and combat the reality of violence and power struggles. When the ability to narrate breaks down or is abandoned, then what remains is the potential for all too real violence to takes its place.

However, in the context of *The Newton Letter*, it is a passing moment. Almost immediately, he declares: "It happened so quickly, with such a surprising, gratifying precision, that I was not sure if I had not imagined it" (*NL*, 58).

The brief gap in his Big House fantasy is closed as quickly as it had opened, but as he says himself, that day was to contaminate everything. He is no longer sure of anything, especially his own conception of himself as the hero of his own story with him as the potential lover of Charlotte Lawless.

One comic moment concerning an elision, rather than a clash, is the final insult leading to the historian's hasty departure from Fern House. He attempts to express his love for Charlotte, to articulate his hidden desire and thereby make it real. His declaration is faltering and stumbling and never actually amounts to much. It does not matter, though, as her response sums up his ineffectualness in connecting with the people he believes he knows so well:

> She stirred, and turned up her face to me, blinking. "I'm sorry," she said, "I wasn't listening. What did you say?" (*NL*, 73)

Soon after, it is Ottilie, as usual, who reveals the true state of affairs. Charlotte, far from being a Yeatsian gazelle, full of silent suffering, grace and refinement, turns out to be quite literally doped up to the gills:

> "Valium, seconal . . . some dope like that . . . She's like a zombie — didn't you notice?"
> "I wondered," I said, "yes."
> Wonder is the word all right. (*NL*, 75)

Nothing he has imagined is even remotely true. Edward is not the wastrel he had suspected; rather, he is a man with stomach cancer living out his last sad days. His actions have no mythic source but are the ordinary actions of a dying man. The historian had indeed dreamed up a horrid drama, failing to recognise the commonplace tragedy playing itself out before him. As Joseph McMinn says, "Formally, the scholar thought of himself as the hero of a romantic drama; now he realises he was only the dunce in a farce" (McMinn, 1999: 84).

He leaves Fern House and its inhabitants behind him. He travels back into a mirror where all those early images of the shy back ends of houses, of drainpipes and clouds drifting slowly over the bay, are now presented to him in reverse order. Very clearly, that sense of his Big House fantasy being cut off from the real world is here made explicit. He has not been able to intervene materially into that world in the way that he had hoped he would. The fiction he made and remade has collapsed; and yet, something did happen. Before he left, he claims he thought of writing a note of explanation for his hurried departure: "but to whom would I have written, and what?" (*NL*, 76). He cannot write to anyone there, but perhaps he can write to someone else. The story of Fern House and his summer spent there remains to be told and he will attempt once again to tell it.

In *Birchwood*, it was observed how the trajectory of Irish history is not a teleological one, that there is no final goal or end to which it moves. History — the past — is, rather, circular and, in a way, always present and asking to be dealt with. Here in *The Newton Letter*, a similar situation is presented in that the historian obsessively returns to his summer spent in the countryside, because he is unable to let it go and move on.

Thus, the first layer of the historian's fiction-making concerns how his literary imagination and how the past — or a certain type of adherence to the past (the historian's over-reliance on Big House literary images and motifs) — excludes a proper and open engagement with the present. The second layer is concerned with the historian's subsequent attempt to find an appropriate style in which to contain all that past in order that it can be re-presented (brought to the present) and understood. It is similar territory to that already covered and discussed in relation to *Birchwood*. The act of writing, then, becomes the focus as the historian juxtaposes opposing styles and approaches to excavating the past.

The novella opens with the line: "Words fail me, Clio" (*NL*, 1). Clio is the muse of history and has been, he declares, his "teacher and [his] friend, [his] inspiration, for too long" (*NL*, 2). Linking her with the idea of failure at the very outset foreshadows the inevitable conclusion. And yet, ironically, after this less than auspicious beginning, the historian starts to tell his story.

On this level, what the historian is attempting to come to understand is why he has abandoned his book on Isaac Newton. Part of that abandonment is due, as we know, to his creation of a Big House fantasy with him as the heroic figure. If that was the comedic element of the narrative, his statement that he lost his faith in "the primacy of text" (*NL*, 1) signals that a more serious tragic note is now being struck. Books, basically, do not appear to bring their readers closer to the truth of the world that they talk about. Humorously, Banville has his historian buy a guidebook to trees and birds, but he soon gets discouraged as the illustrations fail to match up with the real specimens: "Every bird looked like a starling", he says (*NL*, 5).

The historian's anxieties concerning writing are manifested in how his narrative slips and moves between various forms or styles. On a number of occasions he lapses into a "historical" mode of writing so much more formal and academic than the excesses of his "literary" narrative. The tone is aloof and seemingly objective in comparison to the self-centred nature of his Big House "novel". At one point he even goes so far as to insert what is a spoof footnote concerning the presence or not of a bawdy house in the vicinity of Fern House. After these temporary historical interludes, he pulls himself up by drawing his, and the reader's, attention to it: "Look at me, writing history; old habits die hard" (*NL*, 6), or later, "I can't go on. I'm not a historian anymore" (*NL*, 70).

It is not a case that he no longer believes that history and the writing of history deal with fact and truth, just that, as he says, "another type of truth has come to seem to me more urgent" (*NL*, 22). The same was true, he believes, for Isaac Newton. He too had a crisis of faith after a fire in his rooms in Cambridge damaged many of his scientific papers. What the historian imagines is that in the loss of, perhaps, his entire life's work, Newton realises "the simple fact that it doesn't matter" (*NL*, 22). Asked by a colleague what has been lost in the conflagration, the scientist replies, "Nothing" (*NL*, 23). Yet, nothing signifies everything. Newton, the historian believes, no longer knew what to do or what to think.

The "Newton Letter" that gives the novella its title, becomes central to understanding this breakdown. The historian feels that if he can come to some knowledge of Newton's predicament in the past, he will be able to comprehend, or at least begin to comprehend, his own difficulties in the present. In this letter, to philosopher and political thinker John Locke, the great scientist admits to no longer having faith in his absolute mathematical truths, but suddenly breaks off to talk of trips he makes along the banks of the river Cam:

> of his encounters, not with the great men of the college, but with the tradesmen, the sellers and the makers of things. *They would seem to have something to tell me; not of their trades, not even of how they conduct their lives; nothing, I believe, in words. They are, if you will understand it, themselves, the things they might tell.* (*NL*, 50–1)

The letter concludes:

> *The language in which I might be able not only to write*
> *but to think is neither Latin nor English, but a language*
> *none of whose words is known to me; a language in*
> *which commonplace things speak to me. (NL, 51)*

For the historian, this letter now becomes central to his own work as well as that of Newton's. It functions as a kind of mirror, he says, "reflecting and containing" as his conception of Charlotte had reflected and contained the entire world of Ferns. The imagery is significant here. Mirrors are common in Banville's work and are symbols of any system of thought, including art, that attempts to reflect the world. The point being, of course, that they are only reflections and not the reality they supposedly contain.

What is being delineated here is a profound epistemological crisis, in that the language through which we engage with the world is being fundamentally questioned and challenged. Writing and the books in which writing appears do not connect with the reality of the lived world of experience, but only produce endless versions of themselves. The real world seems invariably to be just outside and beyond the scope of language. While there is certainly despair in this realisation, there is to be detected also a note of optimism in that the hope remains that such a language of inclusivity is possible and potentially attainable.

In what way, though, is this letter central to the historian's own predicament? It has been argued that the historian is unable to let go of that summer spent in the countryside, that he is trapped in a cycle of endlessly attempting to discover its significance. In other words, he is, on a small scale, living a version of the Joycean nightmare of history: immobilised in the present by returning again and again to the past, and unable to move on from it. Newton's letter would seem to suggest that such striving will fail, and necessarily so, as language and the products of language will inevitably taint all efforts at true understanding. While he declares that these revelations are wholly relevant to his own position, the reality for the reader is that an ambiguity concerning its true significance remains. This is compounded as the novella draws to a close.

After acknowledging that he had dreamt up a horrid drama which obscured the real tragedy being played out at Ferns; after stressing that, like Newton, he too now realises the limitations of language and acts of writing in connection with the realm of lived experience; after all this, he declares that he will go back to Ferns and that he shall, of course, "take up the book and finish it" (*NL*, 81). He has, it appears, learned absolutely nothing from his own past experience or, indeed, from Newton's past. The end of *The Newton Letter* points only to another beginning, to yet another attempt at understanding. Should the reader imagine that this time the outcome will be any different or more positive?

The short answer to this question is: probably not. The reader can easily imagine that exactly the same mistakes will be made by the historian, that his hope of fulfilling, as he says, "some grand design" (*NL*, 81), will necessarily lead to more tragicomedy along similar lines as has been already outlined. And yet, perhaps there is once more a note of hope to be discerned here because, at the very least, it can be argued that the historian is prepared to start afresh. It is a manifestation of the paradox at the heart of the postmodern condition, of threading delicately between the opposing poles of action and inaction, speech and silence. As he says about returning to the task of completing his book and re-engaging with the reality of Ottilie and Charlotte at Ferns: "Such a renunciation is not of this world" (*NL*, 81). To be human is to strive and the challenge is one of not shirking that responsibility.

In terms of a specifically Irish understanding of *The Newton Letter*, the end of the book raises interesting issues concerning the nature of the past and history's relationship to the present. As with the close of Banville's previous Irish novel, *Birchwood*, an idea of Ireland's past as being inescapable is offered to the reader. This conclusion is presented, as it was in that novel, in an uncertain manner that can be read in either a positive or a negative way. This uncertainty, though, is important.

It can be argued that John Banville chose well the historical figures upon which to base his science tetralogy. The scientific discoveries of Copernicus, Kepler and Newton are important because of their foundational nature. That is to say, these men — each in his own fashion — ushered in the modern world as we now know it. Their influence is not one solely confined to the sphere of science and mathematics but extends to how we conceive of ourselves in this world. Ideas like gravity and a sun-centred universe are mundane truths that are knitted imperceptibly into our lives. Such figures are, therefore, obviously attractive to a writer like Banville, interested as he is in ideas and how they relate to everyday lived experience. But another reason for their attractiveness is that each of them, despite their centrality to enlightenment thought which values the empirical and the rational over all other systems of knowing, actually had grave reservations about the absolute worth of such a system of thought.

It is no wonder, for instance, that the historian declares that Isaac Newton no longer knew how to live after his breakdown. Here is a man whose basic scientific principles still hold true to this day being presented as someone who was willing to let it all go as meaningless. It is sometimes forgotten in the present moment that the "rationalist" Newton — a figure at the heart of the enlightenment revolution — dabbled in the art of alchemy and spent many years actively interpreting the bible. In other words, for the historical Isaac Newton there was more to heaven and earth than all the rules and mathematical theorems he created could account for: there was always something more to be experienced and engaged with beyond the limits of language and reason. This is true also of Copernicus and Kepler, who in Banville's presentation of them, are seen as figures who embrace superstition as well rational forms of knowledge. Kepler, in particular, is seen creating horoscopes for himself and others and on one occasion is observed scrutinising a certain date in the hope of discovering its hidden significance and meaning.

The historian, as we know, also realises that there is another "truth" beyond the facts that history writing purports to uncover. Perhaps what is being prioritised is a sense of "poetic" truth over the mundane verities of the everyday world of hard fact. Certainly, there is an aspect of this to all of John Banville's work. The historian's oscillation between "fiction" and "history" writing could be thought of as a manifestation of this in that it acknowledges the possibility that both, perhaps, are necessary together in order for "truth" to emerge.

However, it can be argued that what is at stake is much more than merely positing the importance of a poetic sensibility when it comes to writing history. Banville is challenging, as the postmodern imagination challenges, the predominance of enlightenment values in the modern world. In terms of history, what is being interrogated and opened up to investigation is the notion of "history-as-progress", that history moves inexorably toward some end point. Taken together, both *Birchwood* and *The Newton Letter* highlight how the past is never "over" and "done with" in an Irish context, that the Irish experience is one where the past is always a live issue demanding to be dealt with.

The challenge for the reader, schooled in logic, reason and coherence and thus believing that a view of this kind leads to chaos and paralysis, is to begin to imagine this situation in a positive and affirming way. Certainly, Banville himself does. It has been observed how he was wont to "play" with the facts of history in *Birchwood*. The same is true in *The Newton Letter*. There is a footnote at the end of the novella which states:

> The "second" Newton Letter to John Locke is a fiction, the tone and some of the text which is taken from Hugo Von Hofmannsthal's *Ein Brief* ("The Letter of Lord Chandos"). (*NL*, 82)

Banville here lays bare his *modus operandi* in a very simple and straightforward way: he will alter the past — exaggerate it, add to it, fictionalise it — in an attempt to reconnect with it.

His is not, then, an art that demythologises the Irish historical narrative; rather, it is an art that demonstrates how myth itself is constructed and is perhaps necessary, along with the facts of history, in order that the past might have meaning and relevance in the contemporary moment. Fact and myth, or maybe a better word is fiction, can inhabit the same space and their commingling can be enabling instead of debilitating. Newton's expressed desire for a new language can be translated into the Irish need for a new language or new form that will adequately map Irish experience: past, present and future.

In a very real way, therefore, John Banville's art connects with that of other contemporary Irish writers. The dramatist Brian Friel, for instance, deals with this exact problem in his 1980 play *Translations*. Set in the early part of the nineteenth century, before the Irish famine and at the beginning of the transition from the Irish language to the English language, Friel acknowledges the need for constantly renewing our relationship to language and the images of the past embodied in language. Otherwise, as he puts it, "we fossilize" (Friel, 1989: 445).

Banville, too, suggests that the task is to get beyond the desire to have a coherent, stable and fixed historical discourse; in the Irish situation, this is simply not possible and probably counter-productive. What is required instead is a constant reappraisal of the past/history to meet the demands and challenges of the present. In other words, amnesia is no solution to the predicaments and demands of Irish modernity; rather, amanuensis — or remembering — is. A radical openness ensues in that nothing is definitely, and finally, defined: boundless potential and possibility are what remain.

While John Banville does not return in such a focused or sustained manner to the concerns of *Birchwood* and *The Newton Letter*, the repercussions of the ideas considered in these two novels are felt throughout his subsequent fictional output. As will be argued in Chapter Four, Banville's fiction after the science tetralogy becomes more occupied with the intimate and the personal, eschewing, in a way, the wider and larger issues dealt with in the present chapter. However, at the heart of the dilemma being played out in both *Birchwood* and *The Newton Letter*, it can be argued, is the plight of the individual in the midst of a wider historical flux.

In Brian Friel's play, the central character, after the Irish place names of Baile Beag have been translated into English, declares: "We must learn where we live. We must learn to make them [the new place names] our own. We must make them our new home" (Friel, 1989: 445).

This is what is fundamentally at stake in Banville's two Irish novels as here discussed. Certainly, both Gabriel Godkin's narrative and that of the historian display the anxieties brought about by an epistemological crisis revolving round a loss of faith in language's ability to connect with the real world of lived experience. The, at times, chaotic nature of their acts of writing are evidence of this difficulty: neither is fully able to control their narrative.

Crucially, though, there is an ontological fallout to these epistemological concerns. Ontology, as a branch of philoso-

phical endeavour, is devoted to the study of being: that is, it
is occupied with investigating what it is to be — to exist —
in the world. In Banville's writing, and in *Birchwood* and *The
Newton Letter* in particular, characters are depicted ultimately as homeless figures. The stories they tell, the narratives they construct, are attempts to conceive of themselves
in the world, and to make the world their own. Even if, as
has been demonstrated, these accounts fall far short of their
hoped-for intention, they are still very much the individual
and unique products of these characters.

So it is with the Irish national story, or rather Irish history. Critics who insist on imposing models of engagement
from elsewhere, or who insist that the Irish past needs to be
escaped from, miss the point that the Irish must approach
their own past in their own inimitable fashion. Not to be
able to do so, means that we are perhaps condemned to be,
as the poet Seamus Heaney puts it, forever "unhappy and at
home" (Heaney, 1998: 65).

It is significant, therefore, that the hero of *The Newton
Letter*, the historian, is never given a name. All his exertions,
in both the literary and the historical spheres, come to
nought: he is, finally, a nobody, denied a name because he
has found no place in the world to be. Ottilie, at one point,
says to him:

> You know . . . sometimes I think you don't exist at all,
> that you're just a voice, a name — no, not even that,
> just the voice, going on. Oh God. Oh no. (*NL*, 67)

Set adrift amongst his numerous fictions, the historian lacks
corporeality and tangible connection to the real world. This,
then, is the predicament of all of John Banville's characters:
to make themselves real in a world of their own through a
less than perfect language that yet holds out the tantalising
hope that a sense of home will someday be discovered.

Chapter Three

Doctor Copernicus and *Kepler:* Art about Art, Books about Books

I placed a jar in Tennessee,
And round it was, upon a hill.
It made the slovenly wilderness
Surround that hill. . . .

It took dominion everywhere.

(Wallace Stevens, "Anecdote of the Jar" (Baym, 1994: 1151))

When we think of "science fiction" as a genre, we might, among other things, imagine a future world of technological advance and fabulous alien creatures. Despite this obviously extraordinary backdrop, the drama being played out is usually all too familiar. Brian McHale contends that science fiction is the postmodern genre *par excellence*, because in its juxtaposition of different worlds, it so obviously brings ontological concerns to the fore. The real world of the here and now and the projected world of the future are imaginatively contrasted so that questions can be raised — as postmodern writing in general raises questions — about the nature of the world and modes of being in the world (McHale, 1987: 59–72). Science fiction, therefore, comments upon the present through a process of estrangement and defamiliarisation. What is familiar and ordinary in the contemporary everyday world is made strange and unfamiliar in the future. Thus, science fiction becomes a means to both look forward and backward simultaneously.

While not set in some indeterminate future, John Banville's science tetralogy, and especially the first two novels in the series, *Doctor Copernicus* (1976) and *Kepler* (1981), could be said to share many characteristics with the science fiction genre. Under the guise of a straightforward historical novel, Banville is able to weave his contemporary postmodern concerns into the biographies of his chosen subjects. In other words, in these novels Banville moves into the historical past in order to comment upon the present. He has said that after writing *Birchwood* he wanted to try to create something other than an "Irish" novel, that he desired to get away from commenting on his own life and his own time (RTE, 1992). Perhaps the uncertainties and anxieties that fed into the chaos of *Birchwood* propelled him toward a retreat from the all too real violence of 1970s Ireland. Nonetheless, the manner in which Banville goes about telling his story of the lives of Nicholas Copernicus and Johannes Kepler sets up a correspondence between that past and the present. These two figures are strikingly contemporary in their sensibilities and, indeed, their scientific discoveries — as depicted — are shot through with the knowledge of present day theories concerning literature. Ironically then, this process of defamiliarising brings out more clearly the problems of the present.

Banville also returns to the past — and to these particular historical characters — because of their centrality in producing ideas and theories foundational to modernity. Certainly, Copernicus's theory of a sun-centred universe is a paradigm shift in thought in that it forever changed our conception of ourselves. We can no longer imagine a time before this, so momentous a change is it. Its influence is not simply confined to the realm of science and astronomy, but reverberates through all levels of our experience. As was argued in the previous chapter in relation to *The Newton Letter*, an attraction for Banville in choosing to base a series of novels on great European scientists was that these men stood on the cusp of the modern world. Of interest to Banville, then, is change and transformation and how it comes about. In returning to these moments of transition in the past, he is able to confront directly the dilemma of modernity and postmodernity in the present.

There is another way, of course, in which these novels can be considered as science fiction: quite simply, they are fictions about science. Science is a common element in much postmodern writing because, in a very real way, the discourse of science is the basis of all knowledge in the contemporary moment. Its claims to neutrality and objectivity and its incessant championing of progress, based on logic and reason, is set upon a pedestal in the modern world. Postmodern writing, quite simply, challenges science's pre-eminence in today's culture. Irish writer Flann O'Brien, for instance, playfully dismantles the primacy of science in such novels as *The Third Policeman*, wherein logic and rationality are turned on their heads and the illogical and the irrational are celebrated. This, too, is a feature of much of Banville's work, the difference being that he never fully succumbs to the inevitable chaos that ensues when reason, logic and stability are undermined, however mischievously. It is as if Banville is acutely aware of the very real consequences of such a loss of faith in coherence and, thus, his work balances itself precariously between acknowledging the limits of logic on the one hand and desiring the comforting stability it offers on the other. It is here that Banville's work raises itself beyond merely the realm of ideas and becomes engaged with the lived experience of the human condition.

The straightforward conceit at work in Banville's tetralogy is that science and scientists become metaphors for art and artists because the problems faced by both are similar. For the scientist, the difficulty is one of creating a system or systems that will actually explain the intricate workings of the world, while the artist also, in creating his or her work of art, attempts to unearth some truth about the world we live in. In juxtaposing art and science in this way, Banville deconstructs the hierarchical boundary between them that privileges scientific knowledge ahead of artistic knowing. He recognises that the human imagination is central to both endeavours and that this at least should be acknowledged. It is, basically, a notion derived from nineteenth-century romantic thought, which placed the creative, or poetic, imagination centre-stage in all human affairs. Consequently, Banville presents Copernicus and Kepler looking both forward and backward in their coming to understand that reason and logic could only express so much of human experience. In these two novels, Banville once again stresses how these characters remained ultimately wary of the very discipline to which they had devoted their lives.

The epigraph to this present chapter is a poem written by the American Wallace Stevens. The poetry of Stevens is of particular importance to John Banville. Along with Rainer Maria Rilke, Stevens is the one poet that the author returns to again and again in interviews in order to elucidate a point or explain tendencies in his own fictional project. There may seem to be, on the face of it, a great distance, spatially and temporally, between Stevens's jar in Tennessee and the medieval world of scientific endeavour as depicted in the first two novels of Banville's science tetralogy, *Doctor Copernicus* and *Kepler*. Yet, the wonderfully simple idea underpinning "Anecdote of the Jar" is the key to understanding what is central to these two novels: art as a product of the human imagination is separated from the world, but nonetheless, functions as a means of perceiving the world. Art can give shape and meaning to the world of nature, though there is a sense that nature itself remains blithely indifferent to all such efforts to know it.

Banville has claimed on numerous occasions that his art is not concerned with self-expression, that he has no interest in telling his own story. It is no accident, then, that many of his novels — *Doctor Copernicus*, *Kepler*, *The Book of Evidence* and *The Untouchable* — are based on real characters and real events. Such a situation offers a ready-made plot upon which Banville can work out his postmodern concerns at a supposed distance. However, on one level, his writing is centred on his own preoccupations and can be considered as a prolonged conversation with himself. His work, taken as a whole, is an open-ended dialogue about art, about its worth and function in the modern world.

The readings of his novels thus far point to one conclusion: art fails, as all products of the human imagination fail, to connect with the real world. If this is accepted from the outset, then why continue to read? One is reminded of Joseph Conrad's character Marlow from *Heart of Darkness* and his attitude to the telling of stories:

> Marlow was not typical . . . and to him the meaning of an episode was not inside like a kernel but outside, enveloping the tale which brought it out only as a glow brings out a haze. (Conrad, 1988: 9)

Whatever meaning and significance a story might possess does not necessarily have to be found in the "ending"; rather, it is the journey to that end point which is important. Thus, in coming to *Doctor Copernicus* and *Kepler*, while both characters necessarily do not succeed in their high hopes of explaining the universe, what is crucial is how this failure is negotiated by the author.

When *Doctor Copernicus* was first published in 1976, many libraries cancelled their order, having believed it to be yet another critical commentary on this great renaissance figure. It is, of course, far from being a historical novel in the traditional sense. Nor is it a book concerned with offering a detailed account of the theories of Copernicus which are, in truth, quite conspicuous in their absence. Nonetheless, the historical Copernicus, and the historical *milieu* in which he produced his astronomical theories, afford Banville attractive material from which to launch his examination of the artistic imagination. Copernicus produced only one book, *De revolutionibus*, in which he proposed that the earth was not at the centre of the known universe, but that rather the sun was the axis round which the earth and the planets revolved. Suddenly, man is no longer at the centre of creation, and is forever condemned to be on the periphery bemoaning his loss of a privileged position. Such a theory in a time of civil and religious upheaval was bound to upset many powerful people. For this reason, Copernicus was reluctant to publish his book, only relenting to do so after many years. His fears were twofold. Firstly, the religious implications of his banishing of man to the margins of God's creation were profound at a time of schism. Secondly, he felt that his theory had no mathematical basis, that it was only an "idea" without any grounding in fact.

While Banville has dismissed as ridiculous any claims for the precise accuracy in his presentation of the life and times of his central character, he does succeed in capturing brilliantly Copernicus's dilemma (ní Anluain, 2000: 30). Quite simply, in a world of chaos, absurdity and turbulence, the great scientist's desire for some sort of order becomes paramount.

Banville's story of Copernicus's life follows a conventional movement from childhood to death and is broken up into four parts. The first section, "Orbitas lumenque" deals

with Copernicus's early life and religious and academic edu-
cation in Prussia and Italy; the second section, "Magister
ludi", is mostly focused on the scientist's troubled relationship with his wastrel brother Andreas; the third part, "Cantus mundi", breaks with the omniscient third person
narrative employed up to this point, offering a version of
Copernicus and his book from the perspective of his student
and disciple Rheticus; the final section, "Magnum miraculum", restores the third person narrative and tells of Copernicus's final years, ending with his death.

It is the first time that Banville makes use of an objective
narrator in a novel, both *Nightspawn* and *Birchwood* being told
by first-person narrators. The contrasting narratives in the
book allow Banville to register more powerfully his own difficulties as a writer writing fiction. Indeed, this emphasis on
form complicates the novel in ways not evident in his other
work. Form now enters into a critical dialogue with the content of the novel; in a way, it comments on the content of
the novel. In other words, "how" Banville tells his story must
be considered of equal importance to "what" the story is
about, reflecting and elaborating on the central themes and
issues in the book. While this relationship between form and
content in *Doctor Copernicus* will be returned to in due
course, at this juncture it can be said that it demonstrates the
development of Banville as a writer at this stage in his career.
It adds yet another layer of engagement and understanding to
this work, highlighting both his ambition as a serious writer
and his skill in actualising his intentions.

Holding the narrative together is Copernicus's theory,
his journey towards that moment of discovery and his subsequent prevarication in publishing his ideas. The title of the
novel, *Doctor Copernicus*, points to one of the more important sources for Banville's treatment of the lives of Copernicus and Kepler and, indeed, subsequent characters like
Victor Maskell in *The Untouchable* and Alexander Cleave in

Eclipse. The source is the Faustus myth centred round selling
one's eternal soul for ultimately finite gain and momentary
earthly pleasure. For Banville, these characters' ambitious
and driven search for knowledge has human consequences
beyond simply their intellectual endeavour. It is yet another
area that links the fate of these scientific figures to that of
the artist who also must recognise the choice, as W.B. Yeats
puts it, between "Perfection of the life, or of the work"
(Yeats, 1985: 278). If the latter is chosen — as is the choice
of all of Banville's characters — then the gains are evened
out with the numerous losses that such a choice entails.
Again, despite the usual reading of Banville as interested only
in ideas, it can be observed how very real human issues enter into his work in crucial ways.

Beginnings are always important in John Banville's writing, anticipating the major themes and motifs in the story to
come. He has talked of writing and rewriting opening paragraphs to get his intention just right, realising the start sets
the tone for the whole work. From the very outset of *Doctor
Copernicus*, then, the reader is made aware of the problems
facing the central character. In a section highly indebted to
the first chapter of James Joyce's *A Portrait of the Artist as a
Young Man,* wherein the young Stephen Dedalus grapples
with the intricacies of language, the young Copernicus, too,
becomes conscious of language and its relationship to the
world it describes:

> Everything had a name, but although every name was
> nothing with the thing named, the thing cared noth-
> ing for its name, had no need of a name, and was it-
> self only. (*DC*, 13)

Before there were "names" there was only "the thing in itself, the vivid thing" (*DC*, 13). In the opening page of the
novel a distinction is set up between the "real" (the thing-in-
itself) and the language (the names) that is used to talk of

reality. It is clear that Banville wants the reader to consider the thing-in-itself as far more important than the words that are attached to these things, for these things are independent of language, whereas language is dependent on these things. As a young boy, Copernicus is aware of this distinction and, apparently, accepts it. Soon, though, this innocence is lost:

> He . . . forgot about these enigmatic matters, learned to talk as others talked, full of conviction, unquestioningly. (*DC*, 13)

From this moment, Copernicus's problems have begun. It is presented as something of a fall from grace, with this rupture between the real world and the world of language signalling the end of an Edenic state of simple acceptance. Language now becomes a barrier between the young boy and the reality he once felt so close to. Yet, language has its attractions and soon becomes central to the young boy's life, cushioning the blow of losing that artless connection with the world.

Language now becomes a comfort to the boy. As he lies in bed, waiting for sleep to descend, he listens to his mother and father talking, "telling each other of their doings that day abroad in the world. Their voices were like the voice of sleep itself, calling him away" (*DC*, 14). There are other voices too, of dogs barking and churchbells ringing: "All called, called him to sleep. He slept" (*DC*, 15). What is the power that language possesses, that is able to seduce the young Copernicus, lull him into sleep in so soothing a manner?

As the young boy enters more fully into the world of language, it is the "real" which suddenly becomes strange and frightening. The friendliness of the "thing-in-itself" observed in the opening paragraphs, when the linden tree's swaying movement mesmerised the boy, is forced to give way to a growing sense of terror as single "things" become joined to other things to make a world of chaos. In his walks with his father through the streets of the town he sees:

> not a world of mere words but of glorious clamour
> and chaos . . . The boy was entranced, prey to terror
> and an awful glee, discerning in all this haste and
> hugeness the prospect of some dazzling, irresistible
> annihilation. (*DC*, 17)

And yet he secretly delights in these forays into the world of chaos, for the journey always ends at the house of "Koppernigk and Sons". Here he wanders through the poky offices, observing grey old men at work over enormous ledgers:

> Great quivering blades of sunlight smote the air, the
> clamour of the quayside stormed the windows, but
> nothing could shake the stout twin pillars of debit
> and credit on which the house balanced. Here was
> harmony. (*DC*, 17)

He likes to witness the chaos of the town only for the contrast it affords him with the harmony produced by the ledgers. Order emanates from language and writing. Quite clearly, it can be also be observed that, for Copernicus, writing can perhaps transcend that breach between language and the thing-in-itself. Certainly it would seem to offer the young boy the hope that this harmonious union might be possible. As the novel progresses, the chaos of reality becomes more unpalatable to the young man, who then retreats into the worlds of mathematics and astronomy, finding in both disciplines a means to bring order to the imperfections around him. The problem remains, though, of how to impose the harmony to be found in these man-made systems on the real world outside of them.

In these opening pages, the drama of Copernicus's life is presented to the reader in miniature. The basic difficulty is how to connect names and words and ideas with the real world. There is a wonderful description at one point in the novel of a character called Nono, who is afflicted with a stammer:

> [He] finished lamely, and frowned, searching it seemed for that last elusive word, the stammerer's obsession, that surely would make all come marvellously clear. (*DC*, 63)

This is a metaphor for Copernicus's own search to discover a name or theory that will reunite the realms of thought and action, purpose and consequence, the word and the world.

Astronomy and the mathematical principles that explain the workings of the universe become his obsession, the heavens being the furthermost point from the filth and disorder of the earth. It is in the heavens, too, that he believes a connection can be made between himself and the long-lost "thing-in-itself", for he discovers that the science of astronomy has for centuries been fooling itself, merely "saving the phenomena" rather than explaining them. Banville has said that the phrase "saving the phenomena" "means a very elegant way of lying" in that all that is being done is producing a theory which agrees with what one sees in the sky but which is not necessarily true (Sheehan, 1979: 79). Copernicus wants to actually "explain" the phenomena, to bring forth the shape of the universe in all its harmonious and symmetrical glory. That is the ambitious task he sets himself.

It has already been argued how important beginnings are for Banville, how they prefigure and gesture toward the major issues to be dealt with in the novel as a whole. Another of Banville's techniques is to have certain scenes and episodes operate in a similar manner, in small and localised ways, encapsulating the essence of the novel's thematic concerns. One such scene occurs early on when the young Copernicus makes a visit to his professor's home. The meeting is not at all how Copernicus expected it to be; indeed, it becomes increasingly apparent that the afternoon will be quite comic in its absurdity. He had dreamt of explaining to this eminent figure his concerns about how false the astronomical project has been since Ptolemy's time, but the ideal and the real on this particular occasion fail to coalesce. There is, however, hope in the image of the professor's daughter:

> he knew her to be an emblem of light and elusive loveliness, a talisman whose image he might hold up against the malignant chaos of this ramshackle afternoon. (*DC*, 43)

From this vision of beauty order shall come, calming him as the house and its inhabitants whirl about him confusedly. It gives him enough courage to proclaim that he believes in things and not names, that the world is "amenable to physical investigation" and that "knowledge . . . must become perception" (*DC*, 46–7). Lofty hopes and high ideals indeed: however, the professor merely laughs at him. As the episode draws to a close, the reader discovers, as does Copernicus, that the lovely young girl in the green dress — the emblem of order amid the chaos — is a lunatic. On the surface an image of sanity, behind which lurks the reality of chaos and madness. It will be the same for his radical new theory of a sun-centred universe.

"Nothing less than new and radical instauration would do, if astronomy was to mean more than itself" (*DC*, 94). Copernicus desires that astronomy become a system "for verifying the real rather than merely postulating the possible". But how is one to break out of a closed and self-reflexive system, referring, as it does, only to itself and nothing beyond itself? The solution lies in a "radical act of creation" (*DC*, 95). It is here that Banville deconstructs the hierarchical distinction between science and art, between fact and poetic invention. He turns our usual concept of the scientist upon its head: it is not the laborious tinkering with figures, theorems and equations that will, in the end, result in the forming of the Copernican revolution, but rather it this radical leap of the imagination. Only then, after this act, will follow the "mere hackwork" (*DC*, 96) necessary for proving this act of creation. Copernicus is now an artist and, not unlike an artist, he can sit back and delight in his handi-work:

> He turned the solution this way and that, admiring it,
> as if he were turning in his fingers a flawless ravishing
> jewel. It was the thing itself, the vivid thing. (*DC*, 96)

The palpable gap that separated the word from the world is overcome in this act of imaginative creation.

But it is only a momentary healing of this division. Once the initial idea has been formed, the problem now facing Copernicus is one of matching the numbers to his idea. It is a question now of writing, of textualising, his thought. The difficulty, though, is in discovering a language that will encap-sulate his theory:

> He had thought that the working out of his theory
> would be nothing, mere hackwork: well, that was
> somewhat true, for there was hacking indeed,
> bloody butchery. (*DC*, 105)

He feels that his idea is being "contaminated" in the working out of it, that it is somehow being lost in a multitude of words and figures which fail to mediate between himself and the planets in the sky. As he continues working on his book this fault becomes more and more apparent to him. Ob-sessed, like the stammerer, in finding that word, that final Word, he goes on to write and rewrite, but:

> instead of coming nearer to the essentials it was, he
> knew, flying off in a wild eccentric orbit into empti-
> ness; instead of approaching the word, the crucial
> Word, it was careering headlong into a loquacious
> silence. He had believed it possible to say the truth;
> now he saw that all that could be said was the saying.
> His book was not about the world, but about itself.
> (*DC*, 125)

His book is transformed into a postmodern self-reflexive
text that refers only to its own inner workings and not to
anything beyond its textualised borders. In fact, his book
succumbs to the same difficulties he had earlier deduced in
astronomy as a whole; that is, in refusing to — or not being
able to — refer to a word beyond itself. He has not united
the two realms of thought and action, as he had set out to
do, and with that the "thing itself, the vivid thing" remains
unsaid. He has stammered and stuttered only, in the end, to
realise that all he can do is continue to stutter and stammer
— there is no word that will make all marvellously clear.

Yet, in the fictive world of Banville's novel and in the real
world of astronomy, Copernicus's original theory holds true:
the earth is not at the centre of the universe. Copernicus is
presented as an initiator of a new discourse. Critic and philosopher Michel Foucault states that a "discourse" is any
system of signs which conforms to certain rules underlying
any given piece of thought or writing (Foucault, 1977: 113–
38). For instance, one can think of a medical discourse, a
legal discourse or an aesthetic discourse, with each having
their own peculiar practices and codes that must be adhered
to in order for the system to be perpetuated. A discourse
then, in this sense, is greater than any one individual who
actually speaks or writes within that discourse. In astronomical terms, Ptolemy created a discourse that endured
for centuries. Each newcomer to the discipline had to be-

come adept in the rules and codes of this discourse and hence, as Copernicus sees it, the falsehood that began with Ptolemy was endlessly repeated within this system. So Copernicus's revolution truly is a radical break with tradition.

If science is a metaphor for art in this novel, then what is being said about art in general and about Banville's art in particular? Obviously, it is a moment to be celebrated by Banville the artist who, without doubt, finds such creativity exemplary. There is a wider significance as well, in that it can be argued that much of Irish writing is concerned with the nature of change and transition. Perhaps it is a condition of a post-colonial consciousness, constantly trying to renew or reinvent the terms upon which reality, and the art which reflects that reality, is to be engaged with. A great poem like W.B. Yeats's "Easter 1916", for instance, contemplates change and transformation, wondering how the rebellion came about and what is the nature of the new reality which has subsequently come into being.

Banville's depiction of Copernicus's act of creation can be read in a number of ways in relation to this issue. Firstly, it would seem to suggest that the truly great artistic imagination can indeed be utterly and absolutely original, and give expression to what has not been said or thought before. Yet, it is a celebration tainted with the knowledge that, as noted, the figures and the numbers do not match up, suggesting that any such fundamental departure from tradition will always carry with it elements of that tradition.

While it can be argued that much Irish writing of the last one hundred years has been highly innovative, it is, in many ways, a rereading or renegotiation or reimagining of exactly that which it was supposedly rebelling against. James Joyce's *Ulysses*, for example, is like no other novel before it and yet, within that novel, there are references not only to most of the great minds and thinkers in the Western tradition, but also parodies of many of the styles and genres of that tradi-

tion. Also, of course, the scaffolding that holds the book together is taken from Homer's *Odyssey*, proving that something "original" can be clothed in tradition. W.B. Yeats, too,
constantly referred to himself as a "romantic" poet, but his
later work in particular can be understood as heralding a
new form of expression.

It is as if to make such radical change palatable, it must
be first disguised in the comforting forms and styles of what
is already known and accepted. Anything else would be far
too disturbing. Banville's own art can be thought of in this
way. His writing appears on the surface to conform to traditional modes; for instance, *Doctor Copernicus* being understood as a straightforward historical novel, or *Birchwood*
being thought of as an uncomplicated Big House novel.
However, as has been observed, he plays with these conventions, extending the limits of what is acceptable and expected within the novel form.

A less positive reading, though, is also possible, in that
Banville realises there is a loss of sorts in this radical act of
transformation. Here, postmodern ideas come to the fore.
The initial euphoria of creation is replaced by the recognition that, perhaps, the promise of change and originality can
never be truly fulfilled because the words, or the numbers,
being employed to "say" this new reality are very much of
the old world. Copernicus realised that, in attempting to
work his theory out, all he was managing to do was move
further away from his initial idea. The same is true for Banville's art, which acknowledges the impossibility of his writing bridging the gap between itself and the reality it so
desperately wants to connect with. Not unlike Copernicus,
then, he stands on the intersection between past and present, tradition and modernity, power and powerlessness.

Copernicus's discovery that he is unable to prove his
ideas is devastating for him. It is also, however, somewhat
devastating for the reader, who is now forced to attend

closely to the increasingly prominent postmodern features of the novel. What becomes clear is how Banville's own act of writing reflects the story as it unfolds. Copernicus's work is seen as "a process of progressive failing" (*DC*, 105) and this is what occurs with Banville's *Doctor Copernicus*.

The third person narrative to this point has been coherent as regards tone and theme. But from the moment Copernicus admits that his project is doomed to fail, the narrative begins to show signs of strain. At first, these signs are almost undetectable, so subtle and unobtrusive are they. Nonetheless, the steady, solid third person narrator who, though sympathetic, has set up a certain distance between himself and the story being told, slowly begins to lose grasp of his narrative. For instance, Canon Tiedemann Giese comes to visit Copernicus in his rooms and during their conversation lets his eye wander about the room, settling on those astronomical instruments scattered about the place:

> Was it with the aid of these poor pieces only, Giese wondered, that the Doctor had formulated his wonderful theory? A gull alighted on the windowsill, and for a moment he gazed thoughtfully at the bird's pale eye magnified in the bottle glass. (Magnified? — but no, no, a foolish notion . . .) (*DC*, 134)

The character's smallest, most insignificant thoughts disrupt the flow of the third person narrative. This begins to occur more frequently, each incursion being marked off with parentheses. Voices other than the narrator's are now being heard for the first time, undermining the authority of that voice. The narrator, too, becomes more intrusive, ready now to engage directly with the reader in a kind of conversation or running commentary on the story being told. All pretence at being objective, of being an invisible guide for the reader, is abandoned. In telling us of how Copernicus refuses an invitation to attend a Lateran Council on calendar reform, the narrator breaks off into this explanation:

> (One may remark here, that while this account — ipse dixit, after all! — of his unwillingness to accept what was most probably an invitation from the Pope himself, must be respected, one yet cannot, having regard to the date, and the stage at which we know the Canon's great work then was, help suspecting that the learned Doctor, to use Cardinal Schonberg's mode of address, was using the occasion to drop a careful hint of the revolution which, thirty years later, he was to set in train in the world of computational astronomy.) (*DC*, 144)

This extraordinary passage demonstrates to what extent the tone and the style of *Doctor Copernicus* has altered from the controlled and ordered narrative technique that has been used from the outset. Banville has said in an interview that this section is based on a musical fugue (Carty, 1986: 18), a definition of which is a "polyphonic composition in which a short melodic theme ('subject') is introduced by one part and successively taken up by others and developed by interweaving the parts" (Sykes, 1984: 397). Certainly this goes some way in explaining the insertion of numerous voices and perspectives in the narrative. Banville himself, however, has stated that he is not overly pleased with the resulting assortment of styles he throws together in this section. Imhof claims that "There does not seem to be anything in the novel to warrant such a sudden, unexpected change into the parodic" (Imhof, 1997: 92).

Perhaps it is excessive, yet it is a practical reflection of the difficulty Copernicus has with working out his theory and how it merely repeats and perpetuates the mistakes and short-comings of what went before. By slipping into parody, Banville acknowledges the lack of originally in his own artistic production, mimicking styles and voices from the past and other genres in an effort to fill the gaps in his own narrative style.

Intertextuality, as has already been noted, is a central feature in all of Banville's writing, littered as it is with numerous phrases and references plucked from the literary past. A good example in this novel occurs with the introduction of the character Anna Schillings into the story:

> Frau Anna Schillings had that kind of beauty which seems to find relief in poor dress; a tall, fine-boned woman with delicate wrists and the high cheekbones typical of a Danziger, she appeared most at ease, and at her most handsome, in a plain grey gown with a laced bodice, and, perhaps, a scrap of French lace at the throat. (*DC*, 152)

These lines are almost an exact word-for-word copy of the opening of George Eliot's classic nineteenth-century novel *Middlemarch*:

> Miss Brooke had that kind of beauty which seems to be thrown into relief by poor dress. Her hand and wrist were so finely formed that she could wear sleeves not less bare in style than those in which the Blessed Virgin appeared to Italian painters. (Eliot, 1987: 29)

In *Doctor Copernicus*, this intertextual tendency has a more serious intent than merely playfully acknowledging past writers. Here it becomes a register of the waning authority of the narrator, tracing his loss of control.

The narrative further disintegrates into a series of letters — the epistolary form — as this second section of the novel comes to a close. The narrator disappears as characters are truly allowed to speak for themselves. The third section of the novel, "Cantus Mundi", sees the introduction of a previously unheard-of character who usurps the narrative. The interjection of the letters and this new narrator brings into sharp focus the act of writing itself, further developing the link between the action in the novel and Banville's self-conscious interest in his own art.

The new narrative that takes up section three of the novel opens auspiciously with the declaration:

> I, Georg Joachim von Luachen, called Rheticus, will now set down the true account of how Copernicus came to reveal to a world wallowing in a stew of ig-norance the secret music of the universe. (*DC*, 171)

Readers of Banville's fiction will know that truth is probably the one element that will be absent from any first person narrative, and so it is here. It is significant that the narrative opens with the first person pronoun and that Rheticus names himself, for the reader learns more about Rheticus and his bitterness toward the world in general than about his chosen subject, Copernicus and his theory of the revolu-tions. Above all else, though, Rheticus is a writer and proves himself to be an overly self-conscious narrator who con-stantly interrupts the text with, not only comments about himself, but also with critical comments on his own efforts in relating his story. His text is punctuated with asides such as, "How skilfully I am telling this tale!" (*DC*, 183), and numer-ous warnings to himself to hold back as he begins to get ahead of his chronological story. Like all good story-tellers, he wishes to keep his reader in suspense and save the best for last. At times he appears more interested in venting his spleen rather than furthering his story — Anna Schillings, for instance, he calls "that bitch" (*DC*, 174), and of women in general, he says, "I have nothing against them, in their place, but I know that they have only to master a few circus tricks in bed and they become veritable Circes" (*DC*, 203). Most of the other characters also fall foul of his vicious tongue.

Despite these features, or in spite of them, Rheticus does succeed in telling the reader about Copernicus and how he (Rheticus) helped in the publication of his book. Yet, much of what is reported is already known by the reader. Nevertheless, Copernicus's predicament, as presented from Rheticus's perspective, is made clearer:

> All the hypotheses, all the calculations, the star tables, charts and diagrams, the entire ragbag of lies and half truths and self-deceptions which is *De revolutionibus orbium mundi*, was assembled simply in order to prove that at the centre of all there is nothing, that the world turns upon chaos. (*DC*, 230)

His theory, then, and the book in which it is contained, reverberate with this echoing absence: truth has not been pinned down. Instead of truth, all that is offered are endless words and texts which move the reader further from that initial moment of creativity. Rheticus's narrative can be thought of in this manner, as can other texts he mentions. Copernicus himself, the reader is told, writes the *Commentariolus* and the *Letter contra Werner*, and Rheticus pens the *Narrito Prima*. All of these texts concern themselves with explaining the ideas put forth in *De revolutionibus*, but at this stage that book has not even been published. This dithering with the publication of the book, and issuing of numerous "introductions" to it, is a manifestation of the "stammerer's obsession". In the end, the goal is not truth, or a tangible connection with the world; rather, the goal is writing itself.

In Chapter One of the present study, it was stated that a metaphor for the postmodern imagination, and by extension postmodern art, is a labyrinth of mirrors, endlessly reflecting one another. *Doctor Copernicus* increasingly fits this model. The plethora of texts that are produced, referring only to each other and nothing beyond, is an example of this. But even Rheticus is shown to repeat the mistakes of his idol. In dismissing Copernicus's work as his narrative comes to an end, he declares that it will be he who shall refute all that has gone before and unlock the mysteries of the heavens. He has learned nothing from his experiences and is doomed to err in similar ways to those who have gone before, including Copernicus.

There is an element of madness to the character of Rheticus and in that, he is akin to the unnamed historian of *The Newton Letter*, who also appears to learn nothing from experience. After the turbulence and passion inherent in Rheticus's narrative, the final section of *Doctor Copernicus* returns to the cool, distanced third person narration from the early sections of the book. It is an appropriate manoeuvre at this stage, bringing the book to a composed end and allowing the tragedy of Copernicus's knowledge to come to the forefront.

Banville has succeeded in bringing together the two realms of form and content, each reflecting the other, and commenting upon the other. As has been established, Banville's own narrative succumbs to the fate of Copernicus's act of writing, dismantling itself as it progresses, with the objectively neutral narrative perspective finally giving way to the highly personalised and subjective narrative of Rheticus. In a very discernible manner, he has linked his own aesthetic enterprise to that of Copernicus's scientific one. Consequently, the conclusions to be drawn from the failure of the astronomer to fully express his idea has profound implications for the reader's understanding of art in general and writing in particular.

Thus far, it has been shown how things fall apart, how art and writing, and ultimately the imagination itself, fail in their efforts to map the reality of the world beyond themselves. Despite this, though, art and writing have a function and a purpose and it is to this we shall now turn our attention.

A crucial factor in Copernicus's failure is that he has been far too ambitious: he has attempted to say everything, to chart the minutiae in order to render the whole workings of the universe knowable. What he discovers is that such knowing is no longer possible. Indeed, an element of Banville's fascination with a figure like Copernicus is that he stands on the crossroads of a world where, as he puts it, "those great beliefs that had sustained man up to the Renaissance — religion, confidence in man's central place in the universe and so on — were breaking down" (Imhof, 1981: 7). The postmodern imagination recognises that grand narratives like these are no longer workable, that all that can be known and engaged with is the local and the particular. There are a number of statements made by Copernicus to his acolyte Rheticus which go some way to explaining what can be thought of as a new blueprint for what art and the artistic imagination should be concerned with. Interestingly, mirror imagery is employed:

> You imagine that my book is a kind of mirror in which the real world is reflected; but you are mistaken . . . In order to build such a mirror, I should need to be able to perceive the world whole, in its entirety and its essence. But our lives are lived in such a tiny, confined space, and in such disorder, that this perception is not possible. There is no contact, none worth mentioning, between the universe and the place in which we live. (DC, 219)

Art should be devoted to the immediate and the specific, rather than attempting to create a work wherein the totality of experience will be expressed. The implications of this are far-reaching. No longer can one, singular perception be privileged over all others, or be imposed upon all others. A universal conception of truth or, indeed, beauty is replaced by notions limited in terms of time and space, becoming fluid and arbitrary in the process.

Grand narratives, however, have their appeal in that they can offer comfort and succour to the human imagination. Again, in conversation with Rheticus, Copernicus asserts:

> When you have once seen the chaos, you must make something to set between yourself and that terrible sight: and so you make a mirror, thinking in it shall be reflected the reality of the world; but then you understand that the mirror reflects only appearances, and that reality is somewhere else, off behind the mirror, and then you remember that behind the mirror is only the chaos. (*DC*, 222)

Art keeps chaos at bay. In other words, it can bring shape and meaning to that which possesses no shape or meaning. The order that imagination can offer is a necessary consolation to the reality of chaos and meaninglessness.

Canon Wodka, a teacher from Copernicus's youth, had warned the young man that science can only explain so much of experience: "Beware the enigmas, my young friend. They exercise the mind, but they cannot teach us how to live" (*DC*, 31). It is a phrase that recurs on two other occasions in the novel (*DC*, 90, 132) and, perhaps, holds the key to finally comprehending the tragic drama that is being played out in *Doctor Copernicus*. Up to this point, what has been presented has been a story of intense and single-minded ambition: a story, as it is put so well in *The Newton Letter*, about one of "those high cold heroes who renounced the world and human happiness to pursue the big game of the intellect" (*NL*, 50). Having entered into this Faustian pact, Copernicus has distanced himself from what is shown to be truly important.

The fourth, and final, section of the novel, "Magnum Miraculum", opens with the great scientist on his death-bed.

His mind wanders dreamily through his past life, as he waits "to be granted an insight, a vision, of profound significance, before the end" (*DC*, 239). He wonders if redemption is still possible at this late stage, for he has always believed that redemption was the "greatest of all words" (*DC*, 66). But what does he want to be redeemed from, what sin has he committed that requires deliverance? It would seem that his sin has been one of failing, simply, to live:

> All that, his work, the publishing and so forth, had lost all meaning. He could remember his hopes and fears for the book, but he could no longer feel them. He had failed, yes, but what did it matter? That failure was a small thing compared to the general disaster that was his life. (*DC*, 244)

All his work has been, on one level, an attempt to erect a barrier between himself and the inevitable chaos of reality. Thus his work, from the beginning, was not trying to explain the real but was, rather, trying to deny it.

The angel of redemption comes in the form of his dead brother Andreas. As a character, he is central to the action of the novel. If Copernicus is said to have spent his life amid the stars, then Andreas as a counterbalance has spent his amid the chaotic glory of the earth. As Copernicus increasingly retreats from the world, Andreas becomes more involved in it, persistently reminding his brother that there is a world — filthy, absurd, chaotically unmanageable — but a world none the less. As the novel progresses, Andreas, more and more, comes to represent the world, in all its grotesque glory, that Copernicus wishes to deny. Like the portrait of Dorian Gray in Oscar Wilde's nineteenth-century novel, Andreas's physical disintegration through syphilis registers both his own dissolution and his brother's desire to transcend the horrors of a hellish world.

What is finally asked of Copernicus is that he accept the world with all its faults, imperfections and chaos:

> There is no need to search for the truth. We know it already. . . We *are* the truth. The world, and ourselves, this is the truth. There is no other . . .
> And this truth that we are, how may we speak it?
> It may not be spoken, brother, but perhaps it may be . . . shown.
> How? Tell me how?
> By accepting what there is.
> And then?
> There is no more; that is all. (*DC*, 252)

Truth cannot be uttered, and yet the paradox remains that language is all we have, limited though it is. But this abandonment of "fiction" is itself something of a fiction. Andreas tells his brother that: "It is not I who have said these things today, but you" (*DC*, 254). Copernicus conjures up an image of his dead brother in order to tell him what he already knows.

The final paragraph brings the book to a close with the death of Copernicus. Those night voices — the churchbells, the barking dogs, the sound of running water — which soothed his childhood bedtime, call to him again, this time to that final sleep that is death: "All called and called to him, and called, calling him away" (*DC*, 254). Joseph McMinn says that this final passage with its lyrical cadences suggests "a surrender to the rhythm of ordinary life" and "return to a perception denied and rejected for so long" (McMinn, 1999: 62–3). The journey has come full circle and is complete.

It is significant that here Copernicus is called Nicolas. Throughout the novel, he has been given numerous names: Nicolas, Nicolas Koppernigk, Herr Koppernigk when in Italy, Caro Nicolo when he is with his friend Girolamo, and Canon Koppernigk when he receives his doctorate in Canon Law.

When he is resident at Heilsberg with his Uncle, Bishop Lucas, he is called upon to declare his nationality but discovers "that he did not know what it was". His Uncle, however, resolves this problem for him: "You are not a German, nephew, no, nor a Pole, nor even a Prussian. You are an Ermlander, simple. Remember it." And so he becomes what he is told to be. He is aware, though, that it is just one mask to be placed side by side with many others. Behind those masks, in truly artistic fashion, is to be found his essential self that no name — be it son, brother, friend, — or, indeed, nation can claim: "He was Doctor Copernicus" (*DC*, 106).

Though he wishes to return to the "things" themselves, he is shown here only to be obsessed with names and naming himself in particular. His final deathbed epiphany suggests that "Doctor Copernicus" is a name that, as with his theory of the universe, has little to do with reality. Like all of Banville's main characters, Copernicus senses some essential lack or absence in his self. The "double" figure of his brother Andreas is a manifestation of this incompleteness: all those aspects and traits he denies in himself are projected onto this "other". By making a firm assertion of himself in connection with his theory — he is "Doctor Copernicus", it would seem that his radical act of creation momentarily brings together his sundered sense of self. Yet, as his theory fails, so does this projected self. In the end, he returns to being Nicolas, simple and childlike with his sense of wonder restored intact.

Asserting this might suggest that John Banville's version of Copernicus's life has been all for nothing. At the end of Rheticus's narrative, he declares that, despite his efforts in bringing to the public the Copernican revolution, that the world is not diminished: "The sky is blue, and shall be forever blue, and the earth shall blossom forever in spring, and this planet shall forever be centre of all we know" (*DC*, 232).

There is something of a truth here. Nothing has altered because the human imagination can only perceive the world and the universe from its own limited vantage point, the rest is mere fancy and speculation. Nonetheless, everything has changed. The epigraph to the novel are lines taken from Wallace Stevens's poem, "Notes toward a Supreme Fiction":

> You must become an ignorant man again
> And see the sun again with an ignorant eye
> And see it clearly in the idea of it. (*DC*, 9)

Copernicus's achievement is that he has looked at the world again and imagined it anew. That is what art, and certainly Banville's art, attempts to do. By calling into question the very language that is used to talk about the world, Banville can, like a poet, revitalise that language, reconfigure man's connection with it in order to continue in the ongoing project of attempting to say the world. In a novel like *Doctor Copernicus*, Banville enacts a human drama wherein the security of the ways in which we traditionally view the world is deconstructed. There is, undoubtedly, tragedy in that loss, but also the challenge to begin again. And this is exactly what Banville does with his next novel, *Kepler*.

Kepler (1981), the second novel in John Banville's science tetralogy series, takes its cue from the previous novel *Doctor Copernicus*. Readers might believe that, in returning to the familiar territory of a Renaissance figure, Banville is merely repeating himself. Certainly, his strategy is the same: he takes the facts of Johannes Kepler's life and uses them as a basis for his continued consideration of contemporary postmodern problems with language and art. Such a duplication of approach and material would surely have been tempting for the author, but Banville chooses instead to challenge himself by producing a work that, while possessing similarities to its predecessor in the series, is on many levels a completely different book.

Historically, Johannes Kepler (1571–1630) continued the work that Copernicus had begun but could not fully master. Taking the idea of a sun-centred universe, Kepler gave it a systematic foundation, making his figures and calculations truly fit the earlier scientist's act of creation. As with Copernicus, Kepler is a man possessed of an extraordinary ambition, who, despite his situation, accomplished so much in his chosen scientific field. He was not slow, as was Copernicus, in publishing his theories, producing many major scientific studies: *Mysterium cosmographicum* (1597), *Astronomia nova* (1610), *Dioptrice* (1612), *Harmonice mundi* (1619) and *Somnium*, a science-fiction fantasy published after his death. These five titles are used to name the four parts of Banville's novel.

Joseph McMinn claims that *Doctor Copernicus* is about "the tragedy of personality; *Kepler* is about the triumph of character" (McMinn, 1999: 65). On the surface, this is very true. Kepler in so many ways is a different character to his scientific forebear: whereas Copernicus locked himself away from the world in order to quietly contemplate the mysteries of the universe, Kepler is a man embroiled in the day-to-day circumstances of life and living. This is a novel brimful with incident, as Kepler contends not only with family obligations to his wife and children and his mother, but with political and religious realities as well. The tragedy of *Doctor Copernicus* is offset in this novel by an emphasis on comedy, or rather, to be more precise, the absurdity of existence. Banville's portrayal, then, is of a man who does indeed triumph in the face of adversity, whose search for harmony and order in his mathematical laws and theorems transcends the seemingly senseless chaos and disorder that surrounds him.

Different material obviously suggests that *Kepler* will be a different book to *Doctor Copernicus* in terms of action and pace, but *Kepler* is also a very different book in the way in which Banville approaches this material. It was argued in relation to *Doctor Copernicus* how he set out to match the form of his novel to the content of the novel, so that the form would disclose in a tangible fashion the major themes reverberating throughout the work. In *Kepler*, this obsession with form, or the shape of the novel, is taken to new heights.

For Banville, form is of the utmost importance; for him, basically, "it is what art is about" (Imhof, 1991: 6). In *Doctor Copernicus*, there were the circular patterns permeating the narrative, as well as the formal disintegration of the narrative in the second section. However, these features can be described, for want of a better term, as "loose" in comparison to the ambitious magnificence of the scaffolding upon which *Kepler* is built. It is Johannes Kepler himself, in a letter to Hans Georg Herwart von Hohenburg, who lays bare the internal structure of the novel:

> I have already conceived the form of my projected book. It is ever thus with me: in the beginning is the shape! Hence I foresee a work divided into five parts, to correspond to the five planetary intervals, while the number of chapters in each part will be based upon the signifying quantities of each of the five regular or Platonic solids which, according to my *Mysterium*, may be fitted into these intervals. Also, as a form of decoration, and to pay my due respects, I intend the initials of the chapters shall spell out acrostically the names of certain famous men. (*K*, 148)

This is indeed, simply and concisely, the structure upon which Banville weaves his fiction. Each of the five parts of the novel represent one of the Platonic solids so that Part One is a Cube, Part Two a Tetrahedron, Three a Dodecahedron, Four an Icosahedron and Five an Octahedron. The chapters within each of these five parts correspond to the number of sides, or faces, that these solid shapes contain. Thus, in the first part there are six chapters (a cube), the second has four chapters (a tetrahedron or pyramid), and so on. Kepler's hoped-for flourish of decoration is also included and by taking the first letter of each of the chapters the "names of certain famous men" are spelt out acrostically; the names being Johannes Kepler, Tycho Brahe, Galileo Galileus and Isaac Newton.

Kepler's favourite theory was that between the orbits of the six planets of the then known universe could be inserted these five regular shapes. It was, not surprisingly, an utter delusion on his part, but one he held to all his life. It tells us something of how he views the workings of the universe, that it should follow perfect geometrical patterns and be, therefore, a reflection of the perfect mind that created it, namely God's. Not only does Banville pay homage to this theory in the shaping of his text, but he goes further:

> All of the chapters [are] of equal length within [a] section. . . . The narrative structure itself is closely worked. Time in each of the sections moves backwards and forwards to or from a point at the centre, to form a kind of temporal orbit. But no section comes back exactly to its starting point, since as Kepler discovered, the planets do not move in circles but in ellipses. (Imhof, 1991: 6)

It is nothing less than a remarkable feat and truly stands as a testament to the writing skills of John Banville. Not once, not even for a single moment, does the narrative step outside of this grand design. It must be said, too, that if a reader was unaware that this intricate formal structure existed, the novel would still be comprehensible, just as James Joyce's *Ulysses* does not become unreadable if the reader is oblivious to the Homeric references which underpin that work.

One of the constants in Kepler's life, as presented by Banville, is his need for patronage and money to continue his scientific work. He is shown conceiving of numerous schemes that will titillate and interest various princes and aristocrats of Europe who have access to hard cash to fund his major projects. One such scheme is his "cosmic cup": a proposed bauble that will conform to the design he had laid out in his *Mysterium* concerning the orbits of the planets and the five Platonic solids that fit between them. He presents a paper model of the cup to Duke Frederick of Stuttgart and is met with the following bewildered reaction:

> The Duke frowned.
> "That is clear, yes," he said, "what you have done, and how; but, forgive me, may I ask why?"
> "Why?" looking from the dismembered model to the little man before him, "Well . . . well because . . ." (*K*, 36)

The reader, too, may well ask this question of Banville: why construct so convoluted a formal structure for his novel *Kepler*?

There are a number of answers to this query. Banville says that, for him, "this formal imposition [is] the means by which I attempt to show forth, in the Heideggerian sense, the intuitive shape of the particular work of art that is *Kepler*, and which was there, inviolate, before and after the book was written" (Imhof, 1991: 6). While he freely admits himself that this may sound suspiciously like "hokum", it is nevertheless obviously central not only to this particular novel, *Kepler*, but to all his work.

What Banville is saying about form should not be thought of as wholly radical or original. Poetry, for instance, can be highly formalised. The Shakespearean sonnet, as an example, has a rigid set of rules and must have three quatrains followed by a rhyming couplet. This form clearly limits what can be said, but also allows something to be expressed in a particular way. Any form, or indeed, genre operates in a similar fashion, both limiting and enabling expression. Applying this sense of form to the novel, however, is important because it disrupts the traditional perspective of a novel's narrative moving chronologically from A to B. It opens up the possibility that there are an infinite number of ways to tell a story. In the postmodern world that we now inhabit, this can be observed in many different media as TV producers and film directors attempt to construct new ways of perceiving reality. The crucial word here is "construct", because that is what Banville is really trying to highlight. Any expression is a construct, by selection and occlusion on one level of content, and by the shape of that construct, which necessarily alters what is being said and how it is received. The medium becomes the message in that how the story is told is foregrounded over the traditional focus on plot development. For Banville, though, despite the form of *Kepler* being, as he says, "wholly synthetic" in that it is imposed from outside, it does not inevitably follow that it is "false or insincere" (Imhof, 1991: 6). Rather, he is making a claim for each work of art, each novel he writes, being unique and thus requiring its own individual shape, which will bring forth its own particular essence.

Perhaps another reason for the emphasis on form in this novel is that it is a means for Banville to try to overcome the deficiencies of language. At the end of *Doctor Copernicus* it may be recalled how Andreas stated that truth "may not be spoken . . . but perhaps it may be . . . shown" (*Doctor Copernicus*, 252). Form becomes an alternative to speech, a means to escape language's limitations. Dramatist Brian Friel also volunteers the idea that language is a communicative dead end in an Irish context, and in his highly successful play *Dancing at Lughnasa* (1989), the media of both dance and music are offered as a replacement to mere words. There is, however, a fundamental difficulty with this reading of Banville's *Kepler*. Not only is the "form" shown, but it is also undoubtedly spoken, both within the text itself in the letter already quoted, but outside the text too, in Banville's interviews about his novel. Despite the claims to the sanctity of shape, words are required to draw the reader's attention to that shape, and thus the problems with language are not so easily overcome, but rather remain a thorny issue for Banville and his characters.

A clue to how the reader should respond to this use of form can be discerned in Kepler's paper model of his proposed cosmic cup. It is intended to promote his theory of heavenly order. He wishes, in short, to reduce the magnificent mystery of the universe to a toy fit only for some prince's banqueting table. The solution to the cosmic mystery, when translated into a tangible reality here on earth, has become a trivial plaything; the real and the ideal do not connect. Banville's intricate formal structure, based on Kepler's grand design, becomes consequently an example of "play" in his postmodern text: a toy-like object to be tinkered with and marvelled at, but in the end only a game to be played by those who care to play it. And those who do play the game can, like the Duke, examine the "pretty thing" in which much time and effort has been placed, dabble "in its innards" (*K*, 34–5), discovering that this paper model is a flimsy ineffectual object waiting to be damaged and disassembled.

Notwithstanding this emphasis on "play", the form of the novel reflects — as the form of *Doctor Copernicus*, and indeed *Birchwood*, reflected — the action in the novel itself, making the characters' concerns correspond with those of Banville himself as an author. This will become clearer as the discussion moves on to consider the action of the novel and Kepler's discovery of his three famous laws.

Johannes Kepler aspires to nothing less than understanding the mind of God:

> God was not frivolous. From the start he held to this, that the song was incidental, arising naturally from the harmonious relations of things. Truth itself was,

in a way, incidental. Harmony was all . . . And harmony, as Pythagoras had shown, was the product of
mathematics. Therefore the harmony of the spheres
must conform to a mathematical pattern . . . It was
his principal axiom that nothing in the world was created by God without a plan the basis of which is to
be found in geometrical quantities. And man is god-
like precisely, and only, because he can think in terms
that mirror the divine pattern. (K, 25–6)

Order and harmony is *a priori* (before knowledge) there in
the world, only waiting to be revealed. In this, Kepler is
shown to be a Neoplatonist in that he believes that there is
a connection between the actual and the ideal, the material
and the divine. It is his task to make that harmonious pattern
shine forth and thereby understand the workings of the
world. His discoveries are consequently, for him, not imaginative acts of creation; rather, they are moments of active
remembering of what is already known.

Kepler's triumph is that he unearths his visions of harmony and order in a world of utter chaos and confusion.
The opening chapter of Part One, "Mysterium Cosmographicum", sets the template for the entire novel. It is
1600 and Kepler arrives at Tycho Brahe's home. He is to be
his scientific apprentice. As with all of Banville's writing, the
first paragraph introduces many of the themes and motifs of
the subsequent narrative. Here is no different:

Johannes Kepler, asleep in has ruff, has dreamed the
solution to the cosmic mystery. He holds it cupped
in his mind as in his hands he would a precious
something of unearthly frailty and splendour. O do
not wake! But he will. Mistress Barbara, with a grain
of grim satisfaction, shook him by his ill-shod foot,
and at once the fabulous egg burst, leaving only a bit
of glair and a few coordinates of broken shell.
    And 0.00429. (K, 3)

In miniature, Kepler's story is told. His mathematical revelations will not come solely from hard work, but from those unconscious moments when the mind least expects it. They will, too, be fleeting moments: the real world and its trials and tribulations will constantly be nudging him awake, demanding to be dealt with. The "ill-shod foot", while it has little to do with his scientific aspirations, points to the nagging reality of his constant need for money and position so that his "real" work can be continued.

As the opening progresses further, the reader is made aware that there is little evidence of harmony or order in the world inhabited by Kepler. It is, rather, an absurd world. Kepler had hoped to find in Tycho Brahe's home a sense of calm and splendour that would echo his own inner desires. Sadly, he is much disappointed. He is met by a dwarf, Jeppe, and the image of a drunken elk which has fallen down some steps, killing itself. Kepler, though, recognises the tumult before him: "the clamour and confusion of other lives, this familiar — O familiar! — disorder" (*K*, 6). Scenes such as this are repeated again and again throughout the novel, establishing a simple opposition between Kepler's dream of order set against the maddening actuality of bedlam.

Yet, out of this confusion and amid the clutter of everyday existence, Kepler apprehends the hidden beauty and mystery of the universe. On three occasions, he is touched by the *a priori* angel, revealing to him his three eternal laws. These are crucial scenes in the novel, with the lyrical style of prose matching the momentous nature of the disclosures being afforded Kepler. That they occur at the most unlikely moments, when least expected, only adds to their significance. The first comes when he is in Graz, teaching a class of schoolchildren the rudiments of geometry:

> The day was warm and bright. A fly buzzed in the tall
> window, a rhomb of sunlight lay at his feet . . . He

> stepped back, into that box of dusty sunlight, and
> blinked, and suddenly something, his heart perhaps,
> dropped and bounced, like an athlete performing a
> miraculous feat upon a trampoline, and he thought,
> with rapturous inconsequence: I shall live forever. (*K*,
> 27)

After months of hard graft with figures and theorems, his
idea of the orbits of the planets and his Platonic solids
comes to him unconsciously. Later, in a drinking house with
Jeppe the dwarf and the Italian Felix, the second of his eternal laws unexpectedly arrives:

> One of the whores fell down and lay there laughing,
> kicking her stout legs in the air. Kepler propped him-
> self against the wall and watched the goatish dancers
> circling in a puddle of light from the tavern window,
> and all at once out of nowhere, out of everywhere,
> out of the fiddle music and the flickering light and the
> pounding of heels, the circling dance and the Italian's
> drunken eye, there came to him the ragged fragment
> of a thought . . . *The principle of uniform velocity is
> false.* (*K*, 72)

Kepler himself is fascinated by this moment of discovery, the
incongruity of his mind working away "in secret and silence
while the rest of him swilled and capered and lusted after
poxed whores" (*K*, 73). The ironic contrast of having inspiration descend in the midst of fetid life in this way is obvious.
On one level it can be seen to offer a corresponding moment
of deflation, thus undermining Kepler's discoveries. Certainly,
such moments in both *Birchwood* and *Doctor Copernicus* are
necessarily undercut, emphasising the ineffectuality of the
productive imagination in an all too sordid world. Here,
though, it would seem that the intended effect is the opposite
and that Banville wishes to celebrate the processes by which
the human mind comes to knowledge and understanding.

Joseph McMinn argues that Kepler is the most romantic of any of Banville's main characters (McMinn, 1999: 76). His courage and determination in the face of numerous obstacles — his lack of money, his lack of social position, his being caught in a violent Europe where political and religious conspiracies abound — marks him off from many of Banville's other, less attractive characters. In short, it could be said that he fits into a heroic mould rather than the anti-heroic space so usually occupied by Banville's leading men. There is, too, his boundless energy and enthusiasm as regards his chosen field of study. Although Banville portrays the agony surrounding Kepler's life — his incessant wandering from place to place in search of a position, the death of many of his children to disease, the arduous labour of his astronomical work — his Kepler is a man who never loses his innocence, and retains his sense of wonder concerning the world about him.

It is crucial, too, that his heavenly theories are revealed to him in the midst of "myriad and profligate life" (*K*, 108). Here, quite clearly, is the single most important difference between Copernicus and Kepler: the latter accepts the ordinary world in all of its chaotic splendour. Copernicus had to deny the world of lived experience in order to create his theories, but Kepler's ideas come from being very much in, and of, that world. Thus, he is a romantic also in his engagement with nature, affording it the respect it deserves and realising that nature is that which he must fully embrace.

The narrative is punctuated with moments of such acquiescence to the secret mysteries of the world beyond himself. Again, these episodes stand apart from the clamour and the confusion that is generally Kepler's lot and, indeed, gain added significance due to their situation in the text. One such scene occurs when Kepler appeals to Baron Hoffman for help in receiving monies owed to him from Tycho Brahe. As is usually the case, he is met with patrician indifference and ignorance to his plight. In the middle of making his case, he breaks off, drawn toward the sound of distant music playing outside:

> He walked slowly to the window, as if stalking some rare prize. The rain shower had passed, and the garden brimmed with light. Clasping his hands behind him and swaying gently on heel and toe he gazed out at the poplars and the dazzled pond, the drenched clouds of flowers, that jigsaw of lawn trying to reassemble itself between the stone balusters of a balcony. How innocent, how inanely lovely, the surface of the world! The mystery of simple things assailed him. (*K*, 60–1)

Kepler finds these occasions truly sustaining, offering him solace and compensation in the midst of the vicissitudes of his life. It is interesting to note how this engagement with nature is interactive in that the image of beauty is both received and created, the human imagination "reassembling" the lawn to best effect.

Another such moment is recalled from his childhood, and somewhat like the Romantic poet William Wordsworth, Kepler is transfixed by this "emotion recollected in tranquillity" or, rather, in his case, this should be reversed to state a "tranquil moment recollected in the thick of confusion and uncertainty". He watches a snail crawl up a window-pane:

> What had possessed it to climb so high, what impossible blue vision of flight reflected in the glass? . . . Pressed in a lavish embrace upon the pane, the creature gave up its frilled grey-green underparts to this gaze, while the head strained away from the glass, moving blindly from side to side, the horns weaving as if feeling out enormous forms of air. But what had held Johannes was its method of crawling. He would have expected some sort of awful convulsions, but instead there was a series of uniform smooth waves

flowing endlessly upward along its length, like a visi-
ble heartbeat. The economy, the heedless beauty of
it, baffled him. (*K*, 99)

The detail and exactitude of this description is a good example of Banville's writing at its best. Despite his postmodern
sensibilities and his anxieties concerning language's ability to
speak the world, he is nonetheless fascinated with the minutiae and trivia — the clutter — surrounding human existence. Again and again, in his writing he focuses in on such
scenes and in describing them gives them a form of life. Like
his character Kepler, he remains bewilderingly enthralled by
nature but never dumbfounded by it, as it forces him to respond to its mystery.

It would seem, then, to be very straightforward and simple; Kepler accepts the world and out of that act of acceptance comes his theories revealing the hidden harmony and
order beneath the façade of flux and confusion. However, as
is ever the case with John Banville's fiction, nothing is as
clear-cut as it at first may appear.

On a close of examination of the novel, the reader
should become gradually aware that in almost every scene of
significance, windows are to found. Indeed, the majority of
illustrative quotations used thus far in this present discussion
have Kepler looking out on the world through a window.
Knowing that Banville is a meticulous author, highly conscious of his own act of writing, mindful of the images he
employs and the metaphors he uses, what is the reader to
make of this constant reference to windows? Quite plainly,
the presence of these barriers, transparent though they may
be, is meant to alert the attentive reader to the fact that it is
not nature or reality that Kepler is engaging with, but a distorted and refracted version of reality as perceived through
imperfect glass.

If this function is admitted, then a totally altered reading of *Kepler* emerges. Those heightened moments of revelation when Kepler supposedly connects fleetingly with the mind of God are transformed. In that first scene, it may be recalled that Kepler stepped back into a rhomb of sunlight. A rhomb is a geometric shape like a diamond or a parallelogram. His idea that geometry is evidence of God's work in the world is important here and as he steps into that light, he is — it would seem — connecting with that mind. But this geometric shape does not occur in the world naturally, or cannot be perceived immediately. It is seen here only through the mediation of something else which, in this instance, is a pane of glass. God, then, does not create geometric perfection, but man through the artefacts he creates does. Kepler steps into a pool of light to ostensibly receive divine inspiration; however the inspiration actually comes from a man very much like Kepler himself.

Kepler himself admits as much in one of his letters from the third section of the novel, "Harmonice Mundi":

> The telescope is a wonderfully useful instrument, and will no doubt prove of great service to astronomy. For my part, however, I grow tired rapidly of peering into the sky, no matter how wonderful the sights to be seen there . . . My eyesight is bad. I am, I fear, no Columbus of the heavens, but a modest stay-at-home, an armchair dreamer . . . [I]t seems to me that the real answers to the cosmic mystery are to be found not in the sky, but in that other, infinitely smaller though no less mysterious firmament contained within the skull. (*K*, 137)

For the reader, if not for Kepler, the conclusion is obvious. In spite of all his efforts to show forth the harmony and order of the world and in doing so, to celebrate man's centrality in Creation (for it is only man, made in God's image, who has the innate knowledge to discern such divine perfection), Kepler has only reconfirmed his, and man's, disconnection and detachment from the world. His only interest is directed inwards into the workings of his own imagination. Like his predecessor Copernicus, Kepler also repudiates the world.

Kepler's character, viewed from this perspective, is not so much one effortlessly embedded in life, as one desperately desiring to be. His cloying craving to be accepted by the aristocracy of Europe is a good example of this, indicating his need to be accepted by anybody, to overcome his isolation and connect with others. But he never gains true entrance into this society and is never at home in their society. On leaving Emperor Rudolph's palace after his first meeting, Tycho Brahe turns on him savagely: "The wrong thing you say, always the wrong thing" (*K*, 84). He does not speak their language and never will, no matter how much he wants to.

Away from the rigours of public life and public humiliation at the hands of the upper classes, Kepler's family life is no better. His wife Barbara frightens him because for him "Women were a foreign country, he did not speak the language" (*K*, 38). From the beginning of their marriage he is unable to communicate with and thereby understand his wife. Though she is portrayed as somewhat shrewish, it is his responsibility as much as hers that their relationship does not work. It is ironic that, after her death, he writes to his daughter Regina that "now, you know, I have no one to talk to" (*K*, 129).

Kepler, ultimately, is never really at home in any situation. His nomadic lifestyle is a manifestation of his inability to put down roots in any one place. Weilderstadt, his family home, is also denied him. On one occasion, he makes a journey back to his homeplace, hoping that it will be a triumphant return after his great success in the bigger world of European science. However, he no longer speaks his mother and brother's language which is comically, yet poignantly, exposed in conversation with his brother Heinrich:

> "You've printed up a book then — a storybook, is it?"
> "No, no," said Kepler . . . "I am no good at stories. It is a new science of the skies, which I have invented." It sounded absurd. Heinrich nodded solemnly, squaring his shoulders as he prepared to plunge into the boiling sea of his brother's brilliance. ". . . And all in Latin," Kepler added.
> "Latin! Ha, and here am I, who can't even read our own German." (*K*, 94)

We are thus presented with two men, brothers even, who at one time were capable of sharing but who now, distanced by language, are barred from truly sharing again.

A recurring motif within the novel, emphasising Kepler's separation from those around him, is laughter. Other characters are seen constantly laughing at him, from his employer Dr Papius, the head of the Stiftschule in Graz, who laughs at Kepler's high hopes for his great future career in astronomy, to the woman he shares his first sexual experience with: "Afterwards she had laughed, and tested between her yellow teeth the coin he had given her" (*K*, 38).

Laughter is an old dramatic device and is used here to alienate Kepler from his fellows: he is an outcast, and different, and therefore open to ridicule. There is also a sense that these characters possess a knowledge that Kepler does not. It is a common feature of Banville's novels to have his main character stand apart and observe other people with their canny proficiency in simply and easily being in the world. This comfort is never afforded any of Banville's heroes, who envy those who appear to be so at home in the world.

The intricate form of the novel, based on Kepler's use of Platonic solids, can now be better understood. It is, to use

Banville's own imagery, a window onto the world of Kepler, allowing the reader to view his life and work, but it should not be mistaken for reality. It is an elaborate ruse, on the author's part, self-consciously calling attention to the fact that all acts of writing, all art, select and exaggerate, not to lie as such, but rather to get the story told in a particular fashion.

Encountering *Kepler* after reading *Doctor Copernicus*, a reader should immediately be struck by the presence of many elements absent in the first novel of the tetralogy. First and foremost, there is an abundance of scientific detail: a reader will come away from *Kepler* actually understanding — to a degree — his theories concerning the movement of the planets and their elliptical orbits. There is, too, a consistent use of definite times with numerous references to months and seasons and years. The most obvious, and indeed comic, example of this is the moment when he inadvertently postulates his theory concerning the five perfect polygons:

> The 19th of July, 1595, at 27 minutes precisely past 11 in the morning: that was the moment. He was then, if his calculations were accurate, 23 years, 6 months, 3 weeks, 1 day, 20 hours and 57 minutes, give or take a few tens of seconds, old. (K, 19)

Fixing time in this manner might give the impression of verisimilitude but it is only an illusion. Kepler discovers as much after promising to solve the erratic orbit of Mars in seven days: "seven days became seven weeks" (K, 63), then "seven weeks became seven months" (K, 64), and then "seven months were becoming seventeen" (K, 72) and finally "seventeen months were to become seven years before the thing was done" (K, 75). Time cannot be fixed, as reality cannot be fixed: movement and flux is the basis of existence and any system which tries to deny this is to distort that reality.

But it could be reasonably argued that Kepler's search for harmony is a search for a system that will encompass this flux, that will make knowable inevitable and inexorable movement and change. Kepler glimpses the truth of the matter when his third and final eternal law is brought to him, as the others were, by his *a priori* angel. He believes the workings of the universe are like, as he says, "a perfected work of art" (*K*, 182). Art brings order where there is none, makes harmony out of discord, but art is not reality.

It is, ironically, Wincklemann, a Jewish lens-grinder, who utters the truth about human perception which it takes Kepler the entire novel to realise:

> An old joke there is, that at the beginning God told his chosen people everything, everything, so now we know it all — and understand nothing. Only I think it is not such a joke. There are things in our religion which may not be spoken, because to speak such ultimate things is to . . . to damage them. (*K*, 47)

There is a world outside language and art, but it will always remain out there, beyond any human attempt to connect with it and make it known. Wincklemann goes on to say that for Christians: "Nothing is real until it has been spoken. Everything is words with you. Your Jesus Christ is the word made flesh" (*K*, 47). Kepler's mistake has been to try to overcome the division between the human world of imperfection and the real world. He has striven to interpret the world with imprecise tools and, finally, failed.

It is fitting, after a life in search of the eternal laws that govern the universe, that Kepler's last work, *Somnium*, is itself a fiction; in other words, a story from the man who once claimed to his brother that he was no good at writing stories. This book has been labelled "the first work of science fiction in the modern sense" (Koestler, 1968: 421). It tells a fantastic story of a boy's journey to the moon and the weird and wonderful creatures he meets there, its creation giving Kepler the most pleasure he has experienced in his long career of writing books. Importantly, too, it allows him to reflect on his life:

> The story of the boy Duracotus, and his mother Fiolxhilda the witch, and the strange stunted creatures of the moon, filled him with quiet inner laughter, at himself, at his science, at the mild foolishness of everything. (*K*, 190)

Kepler can laugh at himself, as others have been laughing at him throughout the novel: now he gets the joke and, in doing so, enters into a shared sense of common humanity that has remained elusive for so long.

So, the close of *Kepler* is similar to the close of *Doctor Copernicus*: a life's work is thrown away, but it does not matter because a new knowledge has been gained in compensation. It is a knowledge that stresses the centrality of fiction, of story-telling basically, to the human condition, for it is only in art — in writing — that the world can be known, however fractured and fragmented are the reflections of that reality contained in the finished work. It does not deny the verities that scientific knowledge can uncover but makes a strong claim for celebrating the poetic, or artistic, imagination which points to other forms of knowledge too.

Joseph McMinn has argued that the tragedy played out in Banville's science tetralogy, and indeed, in all of his work, is a peculiarly male tragedy based on an insatiable desire to know and thereby control the world (McMinn, 1999: 68). Women in his fiction are thus envied by the male characters because of their "composure, their silent strength, their indifference" (McMinn, 2000: 94). They do not enter into the "big game of the intellect", remaining silent instead. In *Kepler*, it is his step-daughter Regina who fulfils this role of silent beauty. While, undoubtedly, Banville can be taken to task for his representation of women, in his defence it could be said that for him, as for his characters, they are, and remain, a foreign country and he does not speak the language. That they are unknowable means that they are like everybody else for the main characters: existing outside their sphere of knowledge, emphasising, yet again, those characters alienation and isolation from the world.

To place women on a kind of pedestal, as a muse-like embodiment of non-intervention and passive acceptance, is to perpetuate another stereotype. Regina's silence could be interpreted in many ways: as ignorance, for instance, or simply as anger toward her step-father. That her presence is open to interpretation is the point, though, because if there is one thing that emerges clearly from both *Doctor Copernicus* and *Kepler*, it is that silence is not of this world. The world demands a reaction. Kepler's final words, "Never die, never die" (*K*, 192), might at first seem absurd, for his own death is imminent (as death always is). But death is also the ultimate silence and to utter these words is to defy that silence, to say anything rather than succumb to the nothingness of the void. Fiction or "saying", then, offers the only consolation possible.

After *Kepler*, Banville continued his science tetralogy with *The Newton Letter* and *Mefisto*. In these two works, he turns increasingly away from historical figures and historical reality. *The Newton Letter*, as we know, deals with a character very much like Banville himself, a historian who is writing a biography of Isaac Newton. *Mefisto* has no such grounding in fact; it is a pure fiction in the sense that it is not based on any real scientist. It is as if Banville could no longer sustain, or was no longer interested in sustaining, the "fiction" of reality that is contained in the first two novels in the series. That technique had served its purpose in terms of his dealings with science, and he moves on.

While Banville's writing seems, finally, to suggest that all is a fiction, that there can be no firm connection between the human imagination and the real world about it, this is not — or need not be — cause for utter despair. Banville has said that:

> I do believe that the art of fiction does deal with the world, that world which in our arrogance we call "ordinary", but that it deals with it in very special and specialized ways. (Banville, 1993: 107)

Fragments and pieces of the world can be seen and can be expressed and, imperfect as these are, we ought to be content with them. We are, of course, never content and are drawn on to try to succeed in saying the world. Thus, in the face of despair, both Kepler and Copernicus were prepared to try again, encouraged with their new understanding. Similarly, Banville, like any artist, must try to reimagine "myriad and profligate life" over and over. From *Mefisto* comes a phrase that, in its way, encapsulates this dynamic at the heart of Banville's work and his thinking about the nature of art: "Cancel, yes, cancel, and begin again" (*M*, 120).

Chapter Four

Mefisto, The Book of Evidence, Ghosts, The Untouchable, Eclipse. Out of Place

> . . . you must say words, as long as there are any, un-
> til they find me, until they say me, strange pain,
> strange sin, you must go on, perhaps it's done al-
> ready, perhaps they have said me already, perhaps
> they have carried me to the threshold of my story.
> (Beckett, 1979: 381–2)

> It must mean something, being here. (John Banville,
> *Ghosts*, 98)

In the previous two chapters, John Banville's fiction was considered in relation to issues surrounding Ireland with *Birchwood* and *The Newton Letter*, and art with *Doctor Copernicus*
and *Kepler*. Looking in detail at only four novels afforded us
the opportunity of coming to terms with Banville's techniques and his major themes. The fiction that follows on
from these works continues in the same vein but, it can be
argued, from a slightly altered perspective. His work remains
obsessed with language, its possibilities and limits in terms of
its engagement with the world of lived experience; and his

fiction is still to be thought of as self-referential metafiction; that is, fiction about fiction writing. Irish themes are also evident, though never so clearly and directly dealt with as in *Birchwood* and *The Newton Letter*.

Thus, while this present chapter will further scrutinise his work in relation to these issues (in a sense, these matters should now be taken for granted in Banville's fiction), the focus of our critical engagement with Banville's novels shifts inward to consider the nature of the self. It could be argued correctly that all of Banville's fiction from the outset has been concerned with the nature of individual identity and how it is created and sustains itself in the world and in connection with others. However, the nature of self and its predicament in the contemporary postmodern world is brought into sharper perspective in the novels that follow *Doctor Copernicus* and *Kepler*. Before turning our attention to the novels themselves, it is worthwhile considering briefly the nature and quality of this subtle shift inward.

After *Kepler*, John Banville abandoned the overtly historical blueprint he had for his science tetralogy. This break with his original design is significant for a number of reasons. Firstly, perhaps, it is wholly appropriate that he did so, for he might have fallen into the trap of merely repeating himself. How long could he have continued to produce historical fictions without his art and his ideas becoming stale by being confined to one specific format? Taking real historical characters and weaving his imaginative fictions around them had served its purpose, permitting Banville to express his postmodern concerns in a particular way. But finishing with that model now allowed him both to return to a type of fiction already witnessed, to some extent in *Nightspawn* and *Birchwood*, and embark on something of a new departure.

On one level, these four novels essentially traced an epistemological crisis, wherein the usually accepted relationship between the world and language, through which we engage with the world, is challenged. One consequence of beginning to imagine language, not as a bridge between the human realm and nature, but as an indicator of the gulf between them, is that commonly held convictions and assumptions are dismantled. In particular, *Doctor Copernicus* and *Kepler* mapped the disintegration of traditional beliefs which had sustained man from ancient times, the centrality of mankind to creation, and religion, for instance, showing them to be "supreme fictions". The grand or master narratives that were once all-powerful and all-embracing are no longer possible in the modern world brought into being by figures like Nicolas Copernicus and Johannes Kepler. One of Banville's achievements with these novels is that he was able to consider these undoubtedly large concerns from a very human perspective. Indeed, this relationship between the big world "out there" and the smaller, more familiar world of everyday existence, was crucial to the tragic drama being enacted in the novels.

His subsequent fiction could be said to embody this knowledge as it moves progressively away from his concerns with the "big game of the intellect" and the issue of Irish history — another grand narrative — toward a more intimate arena for his artistic contemplation. It is a narrowing somewhat of his aesthetic lens, as his art increasingly focuses in on the individual and the personal, thereby eschewing the need to consider the wider issues that he now knows are ultimately beyond the domain of contemporary writing. Thus, the third instalment of his science tetralogy, *The Newton Letter*, as we have seen, concentrates not on a historical character but on a writer of history. This is not exactly new territory, for Banville has always, from his earliest work, been concerned with mapping the individual's imaginative response to the world about him. Nonetheless, a new vista has been opened up taking into account the hard-won insights on display in *Doctor Copernicus* and *Kepler*.

If epistemology has been central to Banville's fiction thus far, so too have ontological concerns. As was noted, the opening line of *Birchwood* reversed Rene Descartes's enlightenment dictum — "I think, therefore I am" — so that unconscious Being is privileged over conscious Being: "I am, therefore I think" (*B*, 11). To be, or to exist, is always prior to contemplating that existence. However, as Banville is aware, the tendency in the western world has been to verbalise existence and to favour that which can be said over that which cannot: "Nothing is real until it has been spoken. Everything is words with you" (*K*, 47), as the Jewish lens-grinder Wincklemann reminds Kepler. Much of the tension in Banville's work is based on his characters' attempts to unify these two spheres of knowledge and make them compatible with one another. It can be said, then, that Banville's writing now deals with the consequences of the conclusions offered in these works, with his novels being inhabited by characters who have inherited a modern world where absolutes and grand narratives have ceased to have any currency. In other words, the epistemological crisis as outlined in works like *Doctor Copernicus* and *Kepler* has ontological repercussions for his characters. Now Banville's primary obsession is with existence itself; it has become, to use the phrase employed by literary critic Brian McHale, the "dominant" structuring device in his novel (McHale, 1987: 6).

It was noted how, in both *Doctor Copernicus* and *Kepler*, Banville made use of the third person narrator, bringing a level of distance and objectivity to the stories he was telling. Of course, this objectivity was challenged and made problematical by the way he toyed with form, in the process making clear that, in the end, all acts of saying or writing are subjective. He now returns to using the first person narrator, thus signalling to his readers that the individual is once again being brought to the fore. If in *Doctor Copernicus* and *Kepler* it can said that Banville as an author or narrator told their stories, he now presents characters telling their own stories. So, rather than trying to understand the workings of the universe, his characters now attempt to come to grips with the more immediate mystery of the self.

To claim that these characters "inherit" a world is somewhat misleading, for a better description of their plight is found in understanding them as the disinherited. The world they inhabit is a fallen one: an uncertain and often bleak place wherein anxieties about man's position are paramount. While isolation and alienation were the lot of Copernicus and Kepler, this condition of disconnectedness is intensified from now on. Though the "supreme fictions" that created a sense of oneness and unity between man and the world have been deconstructed and are no longer accessible, his characters certainly wish that they were. Out of this wreckage, art and the creative, or inventive, imagination emerges, not merely as a form of consolation, but as a means of attempting to begin, in a small way, to heal that rupture.

With the publication of *Mefisto* (1986), the underlying structure of the science tetralogy, already under pressure in *The Newton Letter* where the focus shifted from Isaac Newton as a scientist to a historian writing a biography of Newton, is finally discarded. Gabriel Swan, the narrator, corresponds to no real historical scientific figure as a move toward a totally fictive world is completed. *Mefisto* does not bring to a climax the tetralogy, nor does it neatly answer all the questions thrown up by its predecessors; rather, it is a reformulation of these questions, which as Banville says, "in art, is as near as one ever gets to an answer" (Imhof, 1987: 13). It is, though, a culmination of sorts in that those themes revolving round the nature of the self, in some ways pushed into the background in the previous works, are now brought centre-stage. Thus, *Mefisto* is not the expected ending of the series, but rather a totally unexpected beginning.

The opening, as always with Banville, sets up the major concerns that will be dealt with in the ensuing narrative: "Chance was in the beginning" (M, 3). Like his predecessors, he is a mathematical genius, though, here, his science is never fully explored. That he is a child prodigy marks him off from his contemporaries and his family, making him different from the norm and thus marginalised. He is different, too, or imagines himself as different, because he is a surviving twin, his other half dying at birth:

> I don't know when it was that I first heard of the existence, if that's the word, of my dead brother. From the start I knew I was the survivor of some small catastrophe, the shock-waves were still reverberating faintly inside me . . . The perils we had missed were many. We might have been siamese. One of us might have exsanguinated into the other's circulation. Or we might simply have strangled one another. All of this we escaped and surfaced at last, gasping. I came first. My brother was poor second. Spent swimmer, he drowned in air. (M, 8)

Chance, then, is at the beginning of his life: why did he live and not his brother? The double or twinning motif last seen in *Birchwood* is returned to here, emphasising the divided or dualistic personality that Banville is interested in exploring. A palpable sense of being incomplete, of not being fully present in the world, haunts Gabriel. "Haunting" is an appropriate word because it encapsulates the idea of presence in absence, of being there and not being there simultaneously. From early on, he says, "I seemed to myself not whole, nor wholly real" (M, 9–10). He is separated, disconnected, and isolated from both the world he finds himself in and from the others that make up the world.

Out of these bare essentials, Banville fashions a narrative that expresses his own peculiar version of the modern condition. The novel is broken into two parts, this bifurcation echoing Gabriel's divided self. The first section of the novel, "Marionettes", offers the reader the familiar landscape of a Big House setting. Gabriel is attracted to the strange characters — Kasperl, Felix and Sophie — who are gathered there, undertaking some secret mining project. It must be stressed that, as with Gabriel's own mathematical efforts, none of this is fully developed or explained, adding to the sense, for the reader at least, of a murky, uncertain place where nothing is fully comprehensible. Banville himself has said of the book:

> Yes, *Mefisto* makes many overt and covert allusions to *Birchwood*; I wanted to signal — to myself, mainly — the fact that I was returning to what one might call the realm of pure imagination out of which *Birchwood* was produced. No more history, no more facts! (Imhof, 1987: 13)

Thus, the literary stereotyping of *Birchwood*, and indeed *The Newton Letter*, are accessed again by Banville, but the result is darker than anything that appeared in these two novels. Unconstrained by facts or the need to present a coherent narrative, he can — and he does — offer unlikely juxtapositions and fantastic connections where anything is possible and anything can happen. *Mefisto*, then, is quite difficult for the reader to engage with, as a storyline is practically nonexistent. This is also true for his later books, *Ghosts* and *Athena*, which are also challenging, and to some extent unsatisfying, books for the same reason.

The title, *Mefisto*, plays with the Faustus theme of *Doctor Copernicus* and *Kepler*. The demon figure of Mephistopheles is here given the improbable name of Felix, a character who seems to be in control of events and lives, pulling invisible strings and forever making things happen. He is a knowing character and maliciously threatening as he joyfully bounds through the narrative, slyly giggling at the predicaments of the other characters. He is the tempter, offering Gabriel a chance of life other than his own. Gabriel gladly accepts and is drawn into the weird and wonderful life of the Big House of Ashburn.

Interestingly, as Joseph McMinn highlights, Gabriel Swan, unlike his literary cousin Gabriel Godkin of *Birchwood*, "escapes into the decaying world of the Big House" (McMinn, 1999: 94), rather than out of it. Despite its ramshackle nature, it offers him a place to be as an alternative to his own home. For that is what, essentially, Gabriel is searching for from the beginning to the end of the novel: a place to be.

Although order — apparent or underlying — is from the outset denied, it is the hope of discovering some system that might belie the arbitrariness and randomness of his existence that spurs Gabriel on. Numbers at first seem to hold out that promise:

> It was not the manipulation of things that pleased me, the mere facility, but the sense of order I felt, of harmony, of symmetry and completeness. (*M*, 19)

If the regular patterns of mathematics can be understood, perhaps it will lead to his own sense of sundered self being brought together and healed.

Gabriel's dilemma, then, is that he does not feel at home in his world. His "black book", his narrative, is one means for him to place himself centrally in his own invented world. But he has been aware from his youth that there are other possible worlds, alternative worlds that exist side by side with his own. He recalls his school-days at St Stephen's and his burgeoning dexterity with numbers and his fascination not only with the harmony of problem-solving, but also with the manner in which these problems are presented to him:

> And then there were the exemplars, those faceless men, measuring out the miles from A to B and from

> B to C, each at his own unwavering pace, I saw them
> in my mind, solitary, driven, labouring along white
> roads, in vast, white light. These things, these whizz-
> ing objects and tireless striding figures, plucked thus
> from obscurity, had about them an air of startlement
> and gathering alarm with which I sympathised. They
> had never expected to be so intensely noticed. (*M*,
> 21–2)

What is appealing to Gabriel is that these figures have a task
to fulfil; though it is utterly mundane and never-ending, at
least they have the luxury of a purpose or goal. Gabriel em-
pathises with their plight, plucked as they are from "humble
obscurity", as if he too can understand the desire to be left
alone to continue, unheeded, his own solitary existence.

Another world offers itself to him in the photographic
pictures he finds in the Big House of Ashburn:

> Another world lay all around me here, in a jumble of
> images. How sharp they were, how clear, these pic-
> tures from the land of the dead. I examined them
> minutely . . . as if searching for someone I knew, a
> known face . . . I would not have been surprised, I
> think, if that face had been my own, so real did that
> world seem, and so fleeting somehow, this one. (*M*,
> 80–1)

The past exists as a counterpoint to the present — a world
seemingly more desirable than the present world, more vivid
and unchanging. The presence of this world highlights all too
clearly the deficiencies of his own time and space. The photographs are vivid while his own experience is maddeningly
fleeting; they are more real than his reality.

What these glimpses of other potential realities offer
Gabriel are images of perfection that mock the imperfection
he finds all round him. Banville's entire fictional output displays a fascination with the odd and the grotesque, but never

more so than in this novel. It becomes apparent from early on that almost every character encountered in the book possesses some slight physical impediment or blemish. His father, for instance, is described as having "asthma, and a bad leg", (M, 13) while his Uncle Ambrose's body is said to be "too big for the small head perched on it. He had close-set eyes and crinky hair and a . . . protuberant chin, deeply cleft and mercilessly shaved" (M, 27–8). Not only are his family disfigured or impaired in some way, the world in general is full of such creatures:

> Along with the tower and the broken wall there were the human antiquities, the maimed and the mad, the hunchbacks, the frantic old crones in their bonnets and black coats, and the mongols, with their little eyes and bad feet and sweet smiles, gambolling at the heels of touchingly middle-aged mothers. (M, 16)

Everything in his world is a little askew or off-centre. Although Gabriel appears to be without flaw in a physical way, he too is one of the maimed because of the invisible presence of his dead twin brother, a spectre who haunts his every thought and movement.

Gabriel lets slip an interesting confession concerning this palpable absence in his life. There is a set of twins in his school and he says of them:

> They could have had such a time, playing pranks, switching places, fooling everybody. That was what fascinated me, the thought of being able to escape effortlessly, as if by magic, into another name, another self. (M, 17)

Whereas it might have been expected that Gabriel would have felt some sense of survivor's guilt at the haphazard nature of his existence, this is not so. He does not feel sorry for his dead twin but rather feels sorry for himself, because the absence of his brother means that he has no mirror-image to escape into. It is his brother who should feel guilty for not having lived. What perplexes Gabriel, therefore, is not simply that he is "homeless", but that he is not able, or that he does not want, to take on the responsibility of being himself, of making himself real in the world. Part of Gabriel's predicament is that he would much prefer to leave this task to some other person. The twin motif's implications, consequently, become clearer: it signals the anxieties and the strain of Gabriel having to create and construct an individual identity for himself.

He is transformed into a marionette, a puppet on a string, guided — as are all the characters in Ashburn — by the ubiquitous Felix. The deaf and dumb Sophie puts on a puppet show and the story they tell is Gabriel's:

> The marionettes jerked and clattered, bowed and swayed. The strings seemed not to guide but hinder them, as if they had a flickering life of their own, as if they were trying to escape. It was my story they were telling. (*M*, 114)

He is deeply affected by this display, acknowledging the correspondence with his own condition:

> I thought of the marionettes, twitching in their strings, striving to be human, their glazed grins, the way they held out their arms, stiffly, imploringly, such eagerness, such longing. I understood them, I, poor Pinocchio, counting and capering, trying to be real. (*M*, 118)

This reference to the fairytale character, Pinocchio — the little wooden boy who wanted to be a real boy — encapsulates Gabriel's difficulty. He, too, wants to be real, to insert himself into the world, but balks at every opportunity to assert himself in that manner. Yet, he at least possesses an understanding of his condition. Such knowledge only came to Copernicus, Kepler, and even the unnamed historian in *The Newton Letter*, as those novels came to an end. Here, Gabriel is afforded this insight at the close of Part One. Can he now translate this knowledge into affirmative action and create an identity for himself in this world?

As the first part of the novel draws to a close, the reader might expect that such a transformation will take place. The action winds down: Felix is packing up and leaving; the mysterious project has come to a dramatic and final end with the collapse of the mine; Gabriel's mother has been killed in an automobile accident. His efforts at coming up with some reason for this random event fail. In defeat, he sits back and claims:

> I held my face in my hands, that too flowed away, the features melting, even the eyeholes filling up, until all that was left was a smooth blank mask of flesh. (M, 99)

This death means that the last vestige of this old life has slipped away, the blank face an image of the need to begin the process all over again.

Typically, in Big House fashion, the end is signalled with the burning of Ashburn. But it is not just the house that is destroyed in this conflagration; the photographs and those puppets that so deftly told his story are also burnt. Gabriel, too, is caught up in the fire and his face is horribly disfigured. An opportunity is given, in the words of Felix, "To cancel, cancel and begin again" (M, 117).

The world that Gabriel inherits in the second part of the novel, "Angels", is a world of pain. For a time he no longer drifts aimlessly, cocooned from the events around him. Now every step he takes brings pain and with this pain the knowledge that he is in and of the world. The identity that was lacking in the first part of the novel begins, in the opening pages of Part Two, if not to assert itself fully then, at least, to take shape and form:

> I was alone, no one could help me. The difference, the strangeness. This was a place where I had never been before, which I had not known existed. It was inside me. I came back each time a little more en-lightened . . . I had never known, never dreamed. Never. (*M*, 124–5)

At last, it seems, Gabriel realises that he does not need to retreat into other worlds, nor does he require the aid of other people in order to escape the task of making himself real. He can now, for the first time, take control. The un-bearable absence of his twin, which haunted him throughout his childhood, is finally laid to rest: "Something had sheared away, when I pulled through" (*M*, 130). He is himself now: alone, certainly, but prepared to take responsibility for who he is and who, importantly, he might become.

But, if this is what the reader expects, then the reader is frustrated by the narrative that unfolds. Quite simply, the second part of the novel is a duplication of the plot — thin though it may be — of the first part of the novel. Characters return in new guises: a computer genius, Kosok, going about his secret work, replaces Kasperl; Adele takes on the role of Sophie. Only Felix returns undisguised, as he was and as he always will be: laughing, joking, and turning up when least expected. There is no progression, only repetition; no move toward an end, but rather a circular track round which Gabriel revolves, imprisoned. He does not create himself, but again loses himself in the various roles he is provided by Felix and others. Even the pain that shocks him, momentar-ily, into consciousness of his being is deadened by his con-stant use of pain-killers. It could be argued that a slight shift might be detected from Part One to Part Two, in that moving the action from a rural setting to that of the city signals a movement from innocence to experience. Yet, Gabriel repeats the same mistakes as in the first part, looking for order and shape in the chaos of existence, retreating into the world of numbers and calculations in the hope of discovering some hidden meaning to his life.

Each section of the book becomes a mirror, endlessly reflecting one another rather than any reality beyond their textual borders. There is no coherence, only extreme randomness. In the second section, for instance, as Gabriel drifts through his nightmare world of pain, a motley assortment of characters appear and disappear, never to be seen again. Things happen, but nothing that would advance the plot in any significant way.

It is a very dark, bleak and ultimately deeply unsatisfying coda to the science tetralogy. Whereas the tragedy of Copernicus and Kepler was mitigated somewhat by the epiphanic moments at the end, there appears to be no such transcendence or hope on offer in *Mefisto*, either for the main character or for the reader. Those characters also acted or intervened in the real world, but Gabriel remains constantly at an angle, looking on but never fully partaking in the action going on around him. He is, perhaps, an extreme version of the type that will now inhabit Banville's fictional creations: utterly isolated and alienated, cut adrift from other people and from reality.

What finally emerges from the novel are individual scenes, infused with light and energy by Gabriel's act of memory. It is a common feature of all of Banville's work, but here, unfettered by having to conform to a storyline, these moments stand out clearly and lucidly. There is nothing to connect them with each other; they are, as can be guessed, random flashes of unity detached from any larger narrative that might have given them meaning. On returning from his visits to Ashburn, he begins to notice how the ordinary things around him have been transfigured:

> Things shook and shimmered minutely, in a phos-phorescent glow. Details would detach themselves from their blurred backgrounds, as if a lens had been focused on them suddenly . . . A wash of sunlight on a high white wall, rank weeds spilling out of the win-dows of a tumbledown house, a dog in the gutter nosing delicately at a soiled scrap of newspaper, such things would strike me with strange force. They were like memories, but of things that had not hap-pened yet. (M, 77)

There is a crucial distinction being made here: objects signify something, but do not necessarily have any meaning. Later, in the second part of the novel, another such scene is plucked from memory; Gabriel observes the lights from an aeroplane and is reminded of "a moment from long ago":

> there was nothing in it, I don't know why I remem-bered it, just a moment on a bend on a hill road somewhere, at night, in winter, the wet road gleam-ing, and dead leaves spinning, and the light from a streetlamp shivering in the wind. (M, 158)

Gabriel has lived, he is somebody, but has been unable to create a coherent sense of himself, as he has been unable to create a coherent story.

Mefisto, then, is another of Banville's narratives concern-ing failure. It is failure on a much narrower scale than that presented in either Doctor Copernicus and Kepler, but it is failure nonetheless. Gabriel's scraps of memory offer the reader a hint not only of his method, but of Banville's also. He too can only offer his readership moments, odds and ends, but nothing amounting to a story that might actually mean something beyond itself. Perhaps Mefisto is a failure as a novel in that Banville fails in expressing adequately his intention. Yet, in saying that, I would argue that Banville is aware of this failure. This is a novel about the meaninglessness of things, or, at least, the impossibility of communicating the meaning of what it is to be. Necessarily, therefore, his book will reflect that conclusion and be a manifestation of such inadequacy. At the close of the novel, we are presented with an image of bar-owner Dan's vast "Mammy"; Gabriel describes all the trivia that surrounds "Mammy", all the bric-a-brac that fills her tiny room:

> It seemed to me that somehow I had always been here, and somehow would remain here always, among Mammy's things, with her unrelenting eye fixed on me. She signified something, no, she signified nothing. She had no meaning. She was simply there. And would be there, waiting, in that fetid little room forever. (*M*, 230)

This is the nub of Banville's difficulty as a writer: how to express meaninglessness, how to give form and shape and flesh to that which is nothing? This image of the "Mammy" could, for instance, be a playful reference to the typical Irish mother stereotype: watching, waiting, and ultimately controlling those about her. Yet Banville undermines any attempt to interpret his imagery: it means nothing. Thus, the image of the vast Mammy is completely arbitrary. He does something similar in the first part of the novel, after a long description of Gabriel's visit to the hospital when his mother has been involved in an accident. On arriving, Gabriel recalls a nun sitting at a desk; on leaving, he says she had gone away, but then adds: "No, there was no nun, I invented her" (*M*, 105). Just in case the reader is being lulled into thinking that what is being offered is a slice of real life, Gabriel (and, of course, Banville the author as puppet-master) begins to unravel the entire scene.

The novel concludes with Gabriel declaring that he will go on, that his experiences have taught him a valuable lesson:

> My face is almost mended, one morning I'll wake up and recognise myself in the mirror. A new man . . . He'll be back, in one form or another, there's no escaping him. I have begun to work again, tentatively. I have gone back to the very start, to the simplest things. Simple! I like that. It will be different this time, I think it will be different. I won't do as I used to, in the old days. No. In the future, I will leave things, I will try and leave things, to chance. (*M*, 234)

He will repeat his story once more: a new face is a new birth and a new search for identity. Felix as Mephisto will also return to tempt him in his own peculiar way. There is no closure, no ending; instead there is the possibility of an infinite number of beginnings. Being is denied as a final end or goal: solid and stable identity is rejected in favour of perpetual becoming. Perhaps there is hope in that.

There is a sense in which John Banville took seriously the advice volunteered at the close of *Mefisto*. With *The Book of Evidence* (1989), he goes back to the basics and offers his readers a story at once simple and straightforward, yet utterly compelling. In doing so, Banville gained a popularity that had been previously denied him because of his often challenging and difficult work. The book was short-listed for the Booker Prize in Britain and won the Guinness Aviation Award which was, at that time, Europe's most lucrative literary prize of £50,000.

It is essentially a tale of a murder committed by Freddie Montgomery who, in his narrative, attempts to explain why he did what he did, but not excuse his actions. The success of *The Book of Evidence* has everything to do with the creation of Freddie Montgomery: a character who is at once an anti-hero, yet possessing a quick turn of phrase, and an eye not only for the absurdities of his own life, but also for the absurdities that abound in the world in general. The problems confronted by Freddie Montgomery are the same as those met by his predecessor, Gabriel Swan: his "Book of Evidence", in explaining his deed, might also throw up clues as to his essential self, help him come to know who he is. Needless to say, Banville's fixation with the slipperiness of language and the construction of fictions continues to be at the heart of his writing, but here they can be forgotten by the reader who only wants to enjoy the experience of reading a story well told. In this, *The Book of Evidence* is a return to the fictional possibilities of *Doctor Copernicus* and *Kepler*, both of which had various levels of engagement, from a straightforward story, to the complexities of expressing a peculiar postmodern vision.

For Irish readers, *The Book of Evidence* is also attractive as a result of the reality upon which it is based. In July 1982, Malcolm Macarthur murdered a nurse, Bridie Gargan, in Dublin's Phoenix Park. This event was made even more extraordinary when Macarthur was discovered hiding out in the then Attorney General's home. The Fianna Fáil government of the day, led by Charles Haughey, was obviously aghast at this improbable connection between a murderer and a member of its cabinet. In response, Haughey gave Irish politics a phrase that still has resonance when he declared the whole episode to be "grotesque, unbelievable, bizarre and unprecedented", which, as Joseph McMinn points out, is wholly applicable to the behaviour of Freddie Montgomery (McMinn, 1999: 102). On his arrest, it was discovered that Macarthur had charmed his way into the Dublin well-to-do set with numerous fictions about his past and his position. He was convicted of the murder and given life imprisonment with penal servitude.

There is much here to interest a writer like John Banville: the apparently motiveless act of murder itself, coupled with the figure of a man who created stories of his past in order to gain entry into middle-class society, offering him the material, and the scope, round which he can weave his postmodern fiction. However, it is the photograph of Malcolm Macarthur which accompanied the newspaper articles of the case that, perhaps, holds a clue to what might have been most attractive to Banville about the story. In these photographs, Macarthur is a vision of man out of place, an odd character wearing a bow-tie; in short, not only an unlikely perpetuator of a vicious murder, but an unlikely, implausible character to meet in any situation. He is, then, a template for another of Banville's meditations on the disconnected and dislocated nature of postmodern existence.

Freddie Charles St John Vanderveld Montgomery, for that is his full name, is 42 years of age. He has committed the crime of murder and his memoir will be an attempt to come to some sort of understanding of the actions that led to that awful moment. His narrative is another version of events, as he says, to place alongside the other "official fictions" (*BE*, 220) concerning his dastardly crime. The story he tells is the story of his life, for it is only in presenting the entirety of his existence that this one, single act can be truly understood. He tells of his early interest in mathematics and his desire to be, like his literary forbears from the science tetralogy, a "masterbuilder" (*BE*, 16). Of course, his dream of order, of being "one of those great, cold technicians, the secret masters of the world" (*BE*, 65) is shattered by subsequent events. He meets his future wife, Daphne, when he is a college lecturer in America, though he realises that he loves another woman — an echo of the unnamed historian's dilemma in *The Newton Letter*. The actual beginning of the train of circumstances that will lead to his act of murder occurs on a Mediterranean island where he becomes involved with a collection of seedy underworld characters who blackmail him. This section of the narrative, with its cine-

matic allusions and stereotypes, recalls Banville's earlier
novel, *Nightspawn*. Freddie returns to Ireland to find the
money he owes the syndicate. He approaches his mother in
the family home of Coolgrange, only to discover she has
sold the family paintings that he had hoped would fund his
debt. His "inheritance" has been acquired by a neighbouring
family, the Behrens. He visits them and, while wandering
about the house, is attracted by one particular painting, a
Dutch portrait of a young girl. He steals the painting but is
caught in the act by a maid, Josie Bell. He abducts her, then
viciously beats her to death with a hammer. Now on the
run, he goes to an old family friend, Charlie French, who
offers him the shelter of his home without asking any questions. A few days later, the police arrive and he is arrested,
free now from the burden of "running", and "hiding", of having to make "decisions" (*BE*, 193).

The rudiments of the plot as provided here cannot do
justice to the fantastic twists and turns of Freddie's narrative
and the countless asides, and imaginative diversions that are
scattered throughout the text. Indeed, it can be imagined
that the plot is simply a necessary evil, an example of the
"details" — the hard facts — he is required to produce to
keep the police and his solicitor happy. He is much more
interested in those disembodied moments that together
make up his coherent narrative, for it is there, perhaps, that
he may discover the cause of his murderous act.

From the start, Freddie perceives himself to be the quintessential outsider, cut off from the rest of humanity. Other
people, he says, "seemed to have a density, a thereness,
which I lacked" (*BE*, 16). His life has been a series of roles,
none of which he has taken too seriously. His penchant for
playing has led to his difficulties with the criminal underworld on the Mediterranean island and when things turn
nasty he is unable, he admits, to consider it as anything other
than a joke (*BE*, 14). But when the real world nudges him, "a

world of fear and pain and retribution", he is horrified and amazed (*BE*, 21–2). This detached gaiety in the face of the weighty enigma of living is a peculiar feature of Freddie as a character, reminiscent of the narrator in *The Newton Letter*, and to be seen again, in a different form, in *The Untouchable*. It is a signal to the reader that behind the various masks worn by these characters, there is a void: an absence, or lack, of personality and identity.

Banville gives Freddie's predicament an Irish twist by making him an Anglo-Irish character. Their peculiarly fragmented existence — caught between Ireland and England and being a part of neither — is a perfect model for Banville to exploit in this regard. As Freddie confesses: "I have always felt — what is the word — bifurcate, that's it" (*BE*, 95). Certainly, his father's attitude to his Ireland has added to this impression:

> the world, the only worthwhile world, had ended with the last viceroy's departure from these shores, after that it was all just a wrangle among peasants. He really did try to believe in this fantasy of a great good place that had been taken away from us and our kind — our kind being Castle Catholics, as he liked to say, yes, sir, Castle Catholics, and proud of it! (*BE*, 29)

This quotation highlights a number of things, not least the wistful tone that permeates Banville's fiction. All of his characters, and certainly Freddie, hanker after a better time when all was right with the world. That such a time probably never existed is of no matter, for it is the air of nostalgia that is of importance. Banville is aware how the human mind feeds off the past in order to recreate not only that past, but the present also. More importantly, perhaps, it shows Banville once again returning to Anglo-Irish characters. In doing so, he is recognising the duality and hybridity central to the

Irish condition. Though he is no longer concerned, as such, with a national narrative or writing Irish novels *per se*, his writing does demonstrate tensions in contemporary Irish life. It can be argued that the emergence of his fiction is concurrent with the breakdown and dismantling of the traditional symbols and language through which the Irish expressed themselves. Indeed, as has been seen, in novels such as *Birchwood* and *The Newton Letter*, he directly confronts the issues surrounding this shift. In a novel like *The Book of Evidence* and his subsequent work, Banville deals with the human fall-out of this legacy of disinheritance with an array of characters who exist anxiously in the world, unable to access any shared or generally accepted beliefs that will tell them who they are. Thus, his characters' desire to be real and authentic mirrors the Irish need in the late twentieth century and early twenty-first century to discover new modes of being in the modern world.

There is an interesting encounter that Freddie has with a large ancient man:

> He wore sandals, and a torn mackintosh slung like a kern's tartan over one shoulder, and carried a thick ash stave. (*BE*, 93–4)

The images of a mackintosh and an ash stave point to James Joyce: the mackintosh man in *Ulysses* who wanders anonymously through that text; and the ashplant being the property of Stephen Dedalus. Freddie goes on to say that this character began speaking to him, though "he seemed to have lost the power of articulation":

> Madmen do not frighten me, or even make me uneasy. Indeed, I find that their ravings soothe me. I think it is because everything, from the explosion of a nova to the fall of dust in a deserted room, is to

them of vast and equal significance, and therefore
meaningless. (*BE*, 94)

Thus, in a work like *Ulysses*, Joyce in the very act of attempting to register the significance of quotidian experience actually drains the modern world of meaning by his relentless
effort to give everything a degree of importance and validity.
In consequence, there is no scale or way of comparing what
is significant or not.

Freddie's difficulty is a scaled-down version of this problem, for his is a world with no limits or certitude in any
shape or form: he says of himself that he is "without convictions as to the nature of reality, truth, ethics, all those big
things" (*BE*, 18). This does not, though, offer him any kind of
Nietzschean freedom; rather than asserting himself as an
individual, projecting an identity or self onto the world, this
act seems to be constantly deferred:

> I was always a little behind, trotting in the rear of my
> own life. In Dublin I was still the boy growing up at
> Coolgrange, in America I was the callow young man
> of Dublin days, on the islands I became a kind of
> American. And nothing was enough. Everything was
> coming, was on the way, was about to be. Stuck in
> the past, I was always peering beyond the present
> towards a limitless future. Now, I suppose the future
> may be said to have arrived. (*BE*, 38)

It is in his act of murder that the past, present and future
come together violently, as he asserts himself in that moment on the world.

The murder itself does not take up much narrative
space, but it is round this single act that the entire story rotates, for it is the one frighteningly real moment in Freddie's
tale that cannot be denied nor obscured by his fantastical
and imaginative digressions. Banville's brilliance is that he

juxtaposes this moment of the killing of a real woman with the image of a woman from a painting, thereby showing clearly the nature of Freddie's crime. If science was the medium through which Banville contemplated the imagination in his previous work — catching it in the process of imagining — then painting now takes on this role, allowing him to consider further the relationship between the imagination and the real world. As was the case in *Mefisto*, where Gabriel was enchanted with the possibility of other worlds glimpsed briefly in photographs, painting now offers Banville's character an image of an alternative world to this one, or an image of this world transfigured and made strange through the agency of paint.

His first view of the painting, "Portrait of a Woman with Gloves", comes when he visits the Behrens after leaving his mother's house. He is transfixed by the image facing him:

> A youngish woman in a black dress with a broad white collar, standing with her arms folded in front of her, one gloved, the other hidden except for the fingers, which are flexed ringless. She is wearing something on her head, a cap or clasp of some sort, which holds her hair drawn tightly back from her brow. Her prominent black eyes have a faintly oriental slant. The nose is large, the lips full. She is not beautiful. (*BE*, 78)

Such a detailed description demonstrates Freddie's fascination with this portrait, but he acknowledges that, in reality, he is unable to translate "the fortitude and pathos of her presence" (*BE*, 79) into adequate words for those listening to or reading his account. The word "presence" here is crucial because it is repeated just before Freddie murders Josie Bell:

> She was crouched as before, with her arms bent and her back pressed into the corner. I could not speak,

> I was filled with a kind of wonder. I had never felt
> another's presence so immediately and with such
> raw force. (BE, 113)

Two moments, then, are described when Freddie is assailed
by the presence of another or, in the case of the painting,
something other than himself. There is a difference in response, however, in that the portrait offers him the opportunity to imagine: "She. There is no she, of course. There is
only an organisation of shapes and colours. Yet I try to make
up a life for her" (BE, 105). And this he does, giving over
three brooding pages to his deliberations of what she might
have been like and how she might have reacted to this portrait painting of her: "She expected it would be like looking
into a mirror, but this is someone she does not recognise,
and yet knows" (BE, 108).

Whereas the painting, as he says, demands something of
him — "It was if she were asking me to let her live" (BE,
105) — the brute fact of Josie Bell's actuality, her unassail-
able presence, produces an altogether different response:
her death. It may be recalled that in The Newton Letter the
unnamed historian lashed out and struck Ottilie when she
challenged his authority as a story-teller, saying that there
was much he did not know about Fern House and its inhabitants. That violent reaction is echoed in this moment, when
Freddie, provoked by the presence of another, is brought
face-to-face with the reality of the world, allows his mask to
slip, and strikes out at the affront to all those fictions he has
created, which have, until now, kept the world at bay.

The reason he ultimately offers for this act of murder
highlights the distinction between the representation of reality found in the portrait and the actual reality of Josie Bell:

> This is the worst, the essential sin, I think, the one
> for which there will be no forgiveness: that I never
> imagined her be there sufficiently, that I did not

> make her live. Yes, that failure of imagination is my
> real crime, the one that made the others possible.
> What I told that policeman is true — I killed her be-
> cause I could kill her, and I could kill her because for
> me she was not alive. (*BE*, 215)

Is, then, *The Book of Evidence* a type of morality tale concerning the need to give attention to the real world rather than
the world of art and the imagination?

Certainly, on one level such a reading is possible, for all
of Banville's work is a caution to those who spend too much
time in contemplation rather than actual living. But another
interpretation can be offered. In his fantasy about the
woman in the painting, after she has seen herself transfigured in the portrait, unbidden words come into her head:
"Now I know how to die" (*BE*, 108). It is a curious remark.
Of course, Freddie is the one who gives her these words
and perhaps, they tell the reader more about his own condition than that of an unknown woman in a seventeenth-
century painting.

What is revealed to Freddie is the destructive nature of
the imagination. He has made the silent woman in the portrait live, but in the act of doing so he has also negated her
— as the portrait painter has negated her — because she
has not been the one telling her own story. Thus, while on
the surface there is a difference between his murderous act
and his imaginative act of symbolic murder, there is, in fact, a
deep similarity between the two: he has killed twice. He will
commit another crime in his efforts to make Josie Bell live
again, because in doing that he will only resurrect a version
of her and not the authentic person he has destroyed.

But there is another symbolic death in the novel: that of
Freddie himself. Throughout his narrative he makes reference, as we know, to his impression of being in some way
fractured and not real. He senses within himself the true

authentic nature of his being, labelling this alternative self "Bunter": that other hidden part of him who, like Mr Hyde, lurks deep within, waiting for an opportunity to get out. This he does, we know, with deadly consequences. That single event changes everything, and Freddie is cognisant of this new reality: "In killing Josie Bell, I had destroyed a part of the world" (*BE*, 152). His own little piece of the world is the most immediately affected:

> Everything was gone, the past, Coolgrange, Daphne, all my previous life, gone, abandoned, drained of its essence, its significance. To do the worst thing, the very worst thing, that's the way to be free. I would never again need to pretend to myself to be what I was not. (*BE*, 124–5)

Yet, the world at large fails to recognise Freddie in this act. After the murder and when he is lying low in Charlie French's home, he avidly reads the newspaper accounts of the murder, but, like the woman in the portrait, he is unable to identify himself in the reports:

> from each of their accounts another more fantastic version of me emerged, until I became multiplied into a band of moustachioed cut-throats, rushing about glaring and making threatening noises, like a chorus of brigands in an Italian opera. (*BE*, 161)

The real Freddie is lost in these numerous other Freddies that now roam the earth. But it dawns on Freddie that perhaps there never was a real him in the first place, that these comic versions of himself are merely an extension of the various versions that he created for himself throughout his life. He now desires to be caught so that he can finally be "unmasked":

> And when everything was gone, every shred of dig-
> nity and pretence, what freedom there would be,
> what lightness! No, what am I saying, not lightness,
> but its opposite: weight, gravity, the sense of at last
> of being firmly grounded. Then finally I would be me,
> no longer that poor impersonation of myself I had
> been doing all my life. I would be real. I would be, of
> all things, human. (*BE*, 162)

The old Freddie, who could take nothing seriously, least of
all himself, is no more, but freedom has its responsibilities.
So, death leads to rebirth and endless possibilities.

Yet Banville is aware, as is Freddie Montgomery, that
such essential existence is beyond human grasp. At the heart
of all his fiction, and certainly here in *The Book of Evidence*, is
the idea that life — the act of living — is untranslatable and
yet this is what his characters are condemned to try to do,
over and over again. The real difficulty, of course, is to be
found in language. Freddie's attraction to painting is a metaphor for a yearning to bypass the problems of language and
engage directly with the world unhindered by any distorting
medium. At one stage early on, after Freddie gets his hands
on a dictionary, he muses on the connection between the
world and the language that supposedly maps it:

> I am struck by the poverty of the language when it
> comes to naming or describing badness. Evil, wick-
> edness, mischief, these words imply an agency, the
> conscious or least active doing of a wrong. They do
> not signify the bad in its inert, neutral, self-sustaining
> state. Then there are the adjectives: dreadful, hei-
> nous, execrable, vile, and so on. They are not so
> much descriptive as judgmental. They carry a weight
> of censure mingled with fear. Is this not a queer
> state of affairs? It makes me wonder. I ask myself if
> perhaps the thing itself — badness — does not exist
> at all, if these strangely vague and imprecise words

are only a kind of ruse, a kind of elaborate cover for
the fact that nothing is there. Or perhaps the words
are an attempt to make it be there? Or, again, perhaps there is something, but the words invented it.
(*BE*, 55)

Like badness, Freddie has come to life through language: his
act of writing, his "book of evidence", is an attempt to make
him be. He is still an invention at the end, despite all his
hopes of finally being free to simply be in the world. Once
again, Banville gives expression to the paradox at the heart
of the postmodern condition: he tells us that language does
not do what it is meant to do, but he tells us this, of course,
through language. He offers us other mediums — painting
and so on — but the appetite for "saying" remains paramount.

Freddie knows this too, realising that he has not made
himself "be" in the way he had hoped, that there will be
more stories to tell, more roles to play: "Come on, Freddie,
he said, how much of it is true? . . . True, Inspector? I said.
All of it. None of it. Only the shame" (*BE*, 219).

The two novels that followed *The Book of Evidence*,
Ghosts (1993) and *Athena* (1995), turn out to be connected
to the former and the three together eventually form a series which have become known as the "art trilogy". Unlike
the "science tetralogy", which was planned as such from the
outset, this series came about in much more haphazard fashion. John Banville, in an interview, explains — to an extent
— how this came about:

I didn't think there would be two more books, after
The Book of Evidence; and in fact when I began to
write *Ghosts*, I wrote the first chapter but didn't realise the voice of Freddie Montgomery was going to
come into it . . . [T]hat voice just began to speak
again. And when I finished that book I realised there

had to be a third one. It had to be an arch shape, with *Ghosts* as a kind of central stone. But I'm not sure I was right; maybe *Athena* was one book too many. (Schwall, 1997: 13)

In *The Book of Evidence*, Freddie declared that his redemption would come through making his victim, Josie Bell, live again: his crime, as he admits, was that he could not imagine her powerfully enough — in the way he had imagined the woman in the portrait — and that to do so, to perform this "act of parturition" (*BE*, 216), would go some way in righting the wrong he had done. *Ghosts* and *Athena* are, therefore, the books in which Freddie attempts to fulfil his promise.

Ghosts is a difficult book. Rather than opting to simply present a straightforward continuation of the story of Freddie Montgomery, Banville instead presents an elaboration of some of the major themes and important questions raised in *The Book of Evidence*. In so doing he subverts many of the conventions of the novel form, offering a challenging prospect for the reader who must engage with a work that, at times, borders on being a philosophical meditation exploring the connections between the self, language and the act of fiction writing. The manic bravura of Freddie's performance in *The Book of Evidence*, which insured that the narrative hurtled along with compelling and accessible force, is entirely absent in *Ghosts*. It is a "new" more meditative Freddie, in a way, that is being presented to the reader and therefore a new style is perhaps required to match this new personality.

There is little or no plot to speak of; the only real "action" in the novel being the description of Freddie's journey to the island after he has been released from prison. It is, therefore, quite static, possessing an air of quiet, dreamlike inertness. The title of the novel, *Ghosts*, implies as much, suggesting that a sense of otherworldliness as well as of haunting is central to the text. In consequence, the world conjured up for the reader is a perplexingly twilight one, wherein events and characters are only half-seen and half-understood. In truth, it is hardly a novel at all in the traditional sense. Like Freddie, who wants to be real, *Ghosts* itself strives to be a real novel. This should not be thought of as a criticism, because, as always with John Banville, there is purpose and conscious intention to his artistic sleights of hand.

Ten years have passed since Freddie's crime; he has been released from prison and now lives on an island off the coast of Ireland. He has found a position, appropriately enough, with an art historian, the withdrawn Professor Kreutznaer and shares his home, along with Licht, who occupies an indefinite role of cook, maid and gardener. It is a novel of four parts. The first part begins, in imitation of the epic form, in *media res*, with the accidental arrival of an assorted troupe of day-trippers from the mainland. This first lengthy section is given over to a very disjointed and disorienting account of these characters and their disruptive presence among Freddie and his companions. With the second section, Freddie's narrative moves back in time and tells of his departure from prison and his journey to the island. The third section is brief and taken up with a description, by Freddie, of a painting, "Le Monde d'Or", by the artist Vaublin — which is a playful version of the name Banville. This painting is significant, in that its shadowy presence is felt throughout the narrative and it could be said that, in the absence of a plot, it is one of the more obvious unifying forces holding the threadbare narrative together. The fourth and final part brings the reader back to the present and offers a conclusion of sorts.

Within this framework, nothing much occurs — things do happen, characters meet each other, interact and have conversations, but ultimately to no great end. Certainly, in the first long section of the novel — it takes up over half of the book — there appears to be no coherent structure giving reason to what is being presented. The book opens with the arrival of a motley crew of tourists scrambling ashore after their pleasure boat has run aground:

> Here they are. There are seven of them. Or better say, half a dozen or so, that gives more leeway. They are struggling up the dunes, stumbling in the sand, squabbling, complaining, wanting sympathy, wanting to be elsewhere. There is no elsewhere, for them. Only here, in this little round. (*G*, 3)

As if emphasising the casual nature of what will unfold, these characters are brought to the island by an accident, the drunken pilot of the boat having run the pleasure cruiser aground. The theatricality of this scene, with its self-referential allusion to the "round", along with the slight process of revision regarding the desire for a lack of exactness as to their number, suggests something of a performance. But precisely who is performing? And for whom? The answer comes soon after:

> Thus things begin. It is a morning late in May. The sun shines merrily. How the wind blows! A little world is coming to being.
>   Who speaks? I do. Little God. (*G*, 3–4)

From the very outset, the narrative's fictionality is being stressed: it is an improvised act of creation on the part of the narrator who, at this early stage, the reader does not yet know is Freddie Montgomery.

Freddie's narrative reverberates with echoes of numerous other texts, most notably in this early section, with its survivors of a shipwreck, to William Shakespeare's last play, *The Tempest*. But there are allusions also to Banville's own earlier fiction. The diabolical Felix, last seen in *Mefisto*, returns as Gabriel Swan said he would, still impishly playful and knowing — it is he who recognises Freddie — though, overall, he is a much more benign figure than he was in his previous incarnation. In general, the languorous prose, displaying a painterly eye for detail, is employed for no real purpose because nothing happens of any great interest or import. Indeed, the numerous pen pictures of the characters as they wander aimlessly about the island have the quality of painting: there is no narrative theme holding them together in a novelistic sense; they are simply single elements — parts — of a picture that can only be apprehended as a whole. No one character rises above another to a level of importance that would hold the reader's attention. Each episode melts into the others as the controlling narrator's eye flits back and forth between them, lingering for a moment but never lingering for too long. The overwhelming effect is one of the text being haunted. These characters are ghosts from other fictions, out of place on the island, out of place in this story; and, taken out of their proper *milieu*, destined to be spectre-like and never fully present within it.

Ghosts, of course, only become fully present in the eye of the beholder in the meeting of the supernatural world and the real world. The same is true here. While the characters themselves remain curiously passive throughout, in contrast what is active is this creative imagination of the narrator — the little God — who animates all about him. A key passage in this first section hints at what is at stake:

> Nothing happens, nothing will happen, yet everything is poised, waiting . . . This is what holds it together, this sense of expectancy, like a spring tensed in mid-air and sustained by its own force, exerting equal force everywhere. And I, I am there and not there: I am the pretext of things . . . Without me there would be no moment, no separable event, only the

brute, blind drift of things. That seems true; important, too. (G, 40)

The narrative is not concerned with these other characters in and of themselves; rather, it is concerned with the position of the narrator, that is Freddie, in relation to this narrative which he is telling. In making these characters live, he discovers that he is required, that he has a purpose. There is a moment when he tells us of his attraction to plants and gardening:

> I have a notion, foolish, I know, that it is because of me that they cling on, that my ministrations, no simply my presence gives them heart somehow, and makes them live. Who or what would there be to notice their struggles if I did not come out and walk among them every day? It must mean something, being here. I am the agent of individuation: in me they find their singularity. (G, 98)

He could be talking about the assembled characters on the island and his crucial presence in giving them existence. Still, his own sense of self is not yet fully realised in this act, for he says:

> And yet, though I am one of them, I am only half a figure, a figure half-seen, standing in the doorway, or sitting at a corner of the scrubbed pine table with a cracked mug at my elbow, and if they try to see me straight, or turn their heads too quickly, I am gone. (G, 40)

Freddie is, therefore, something of a ghost himself. It becomes clearer that the unfolding story's real subject is Freddie himself. His interest in the characters is their similarity to himself: "Somehow these people looked like him, like the image he had of himself: lost, eager, ill at ease and foolish" (*G*, 10).

In telling, or trying to tell, their story, he is attempting to tell his own. Freddie's problem is still unresolved and his overwhelming sense of alienation and displacement in and from the world remains. He had hoped that in writing his first "book of evidence" to dispel this "weightlessness" and ground himself in words. It did not happen then and does not happen now.

The entire novel, and certainly, this first part of it, is like an elaborate ruse or joke. All of it, or none of it, happens. Perhaps it is a dream of Freddie's, still locked away in prison and imagining another life, another world. It is not so apparent on a first reading, but on a second and subsequent readings the provisionality of the text becomes conspicuous. Freddie talks about "his" creatures — his creations — and how he might just leave them there, suspended in mid-sentence. He forces himself to continue with the narrative, every now and then spurring himself on to talk about the finer points of tea, or offer an informative digression on the nature of ghosts. Certain words appear again and again; for instance, plausible and implausible, registering Freddie's (and indeed Banville's) awareness of the less than convincing nature of the text. As Freddie points out: all is expectancy, with objects and characters in limbo, waiting for something to happen. It is as if what is being offered here are the rudiments, the bare essentials, of a story — or a number of stories — that might be told in the future. The reader is privy to a work-in-progress of a novel that is yet to be.

Banville has said that he imagines Freddie inhabiting purgatory and is thus caught between the living and the dead, imagination and reality (Schwall, 1997: 14). What he is attempting to do in his manipulation of these characters is to create a world that not only they can be in, but that he can be in also. He needs desperately to impose himself upon this world, to give his wraith-like self substance. Needless to say, he is wrong.

One of the raggle-taggle band of travellers is a girl called Flora. She, too, is reminiscent of previous characters in Banville's fiction. Here, she reminds Freddie of that other young woman, Josie Bell, who he said he had to recreate and make live in his imagination. When the others leave, Flora decides to stay on the island. The first part of the novel comes to a close with this information and with a significant encounter between Freddie and his new guest:

> And as she talked I found myself looking at her and seeing her as if for the first time, not as a gathering of details, but all of a piece, solid and singular and amazing . . . She was simply there, an incarnation of herself, no longer a nexus of adjectives but pure and present noun . . . No longer Our Lady of the Enigmas, but a girl, just a girl. (G, 147)

In the presence of this woman — as she is, with no elaboration from his creative imagination — he realises that this is what he had been after all along. In losing himself, in accepting Flora simply for what she is, he can, paradoxically, find himself. The moment resonates with possibility for Freddie:

> And somehow by being suddenly herself like this she made the things about her be there too. In her, and in what she spoke, the world, the little world in which we sat, found its grounding and was realised. . . . I felt everyone and everything shiver and shift, falling into vividest forms, detaching themselves from me and my conception of them and changing themselves instead into what they were, no longer figment, no longer mystery, no longer a part of my imagining. And I, was I there amongst them, at last? (G, 147)

With this tentative question he appears to hold out the possibility that he has finally entered into the world, that he is no longer the controlling God of the characters, but their equal.

Yet, as is always the case with Banville's work, there is no end to the imagination's engagement with the world and thus this moment of revelation is undercut by the continuing narrative. The story shifts back in time in the second section, regressing to tell the story of Freddie's departure from prison and his arrival on the island. He makes a detour to his home but realises that his future is not to be found there in his old life. The nature of his new-found freedom is a daunting prospect:

> I am free, I told myself, but what does it signify? The objectless liberty is a burden to me. Forget the past, then, give up all hope of retrieving my lost selves, just let go, just let it all fade away. And then be something new . . . Was that it, that I must imagine myself into existence before tackling the harder task of conjuring another? (*G*, 195–6)

Freddie articulates his purgatorial state: there is no past for him to return to, and the future is yet to be, but only if he can create and sustain a viable sense of himself. That is the predicament and the challenge that has been worked out in the first part of the novel. It was Freddie's attempt to project a world with himself at the heart of it.

Part three of *Ghosts* is a brief meditation on Vaublin's painting "Le Monde d'Or". Freddie is still the narrator, though now he shifts into slightly scholarly style and tone. The painting which Freddie contemplates is an amalgam of three famous paintings by the French artist Watteau (1684–1721): "Pierrot, dit autrefois Gilles", which foregrounds a clown figure; and the artist's two versions of "Pilgrimage to Cythere", Cythere being the island of love (McMinn, 1999:

123–7). The painting and the painter, "Vaublin", have been a ghostly presence throughout the text, especially in the first section of the novel. Now, however, this picture is clearly presented to the reader:

> He stands before us like our own reflection distorted in a mirror, known yet strange. What is he doing here, on this raised ground, in this glided inexplicable light? He is isolated from the rest of the figures ranged round him, suspended between their world and ours. (G, 225)

In these opening lines it can be argued that Freddie gives the game away, as it were. The key to understanding the intricate joke that is *Ghosts* is here offered to the reader. The use of the scholarly "we" should not disguise the fact that it is Freddie who sees himself reflected in this work of art: he is the figure set apart, alone and isolated, who in a mysterious manner appears to be part of neither our world or the world of fiction. He goes on:

> It is first of all a masterpiece of pure composition, of the architectonic arrangement of light and shade, of earth and sky, of presence and absence, and yet we cannot prevent ourselves asking what it is that gives the scene its air of mystery and profound and at the same time playful significance. Who are these people? we ask, for it seems to matter not what they may be doing, but what they are. (G, 227–8)

Quite simply it is a commentary on the book *Ghosts* itself — capturing wonderfully its essence better than any critic or reviewer might. Many of the shipwrecked pleasure-seekers find their source in the painting: Croke the actor, Felix the malevolent and knowing presence, the two boys, and, in the figure of the clown, Freddie himself: they are all there. The static nature that prevailed in the first part is also explained:

What happens does not matter; the moment is all. This is the golden world. The painter has gathered his little group and set them down in this wind-tossed glade, in this delicate, artificial light, and painted them as angels and as clowns. It is a world where yet the mystery of things is preserved; a world where they may live, however briefly, however tenuously, in the failing evening of the self, solitary and at the same time together somehow here in this place, dying as they may be and yet fixed forever in a luminous, unending instant. (G, 231)

Typically, Freddie's prose rises to the level of poetry in this description of the painting. In contrast, his version of the "the Golden World", while containing glimpses of this original version, failed to sustain itself or hang so coherently together. Banville has said his favourite book of the art trilogy is *Ghosts* because it is "such a failure" (Schwall, 1997: 13). It fails because Freddie Montgomery fails to construct a world as bright and as meaningful as the template he chooses to base it on. It is a pale imitation of this original. He has, in short, been unable to reimagine himself convincingly into the real world of nature and of others.

And yet, the situation is not as cut and dried as it might seem. The shadowy presence of "Le Monde d'Or" underpins the action — or lack of it — in the novel, but so does its creator, Vaublin. There are numerous digressions offering what little details of his life and career that are known:

Even his name is uncertain: Faubelin, Vanhoblin, Van Hobellijn? Take your pick. He changed his name, his nationality, everything, covering his tracks . . . Yes, a manufactured man. (G, 35)

Did Vaublin achieve what Freddie has not? Did he invent himself anew and did this "new" man then produce the painting? Possibly, or possibly not. It turns out that the painting's provenance is not assured. In other words, it is not an original but a fake. Of course, it is Felix who possesses this knowledge and passes it on to Freddie, who is now left to muse:

> If this is a fake, what then would be the genuine thing? And if Vaublin did not paint it, who did? . . . My writing is almost done: Vaublin shall live! If you call this life. He too was no more than a copy, of his own self. As I am, of mine. (*G*, 245)

In a sense, Freddie gets lost here, slipping out of sight of the numerous reflecting mirrors in the text, and the endless literary game playing being employed. Perhaps, though, there is a real revelation being presented at the close of the novel, a revelation that is at the heart, not only of this novel, but of all of Banville's work. His writing from the beginning of his career has oscillated between the poles of truth and fiction, art and reality. He has shown himself acutely aware of the delicate balance in the relationship that the human intellect has with the world of nature and reality, having his characters constantly attempting to bridge the gap between the two realms of experience. There are moments in all of his writing when such a union appears possible, and yet he undermines these brief glimpses in a variety of ways, as we have observed. The problem centres around that human construct, language, which — in Banville's fiction — singularly fails to represent the world adequately. Near the end of *Ghosts*, Freddie complains that, after all his effort, he has accomplished nothing:

> Some incarnation this is. I have achieved nothing, nothing. I am what I always was, alone as always, locked in the same old glass prison of myself. (*G*, 236)

Unable to connect with the world beyond himself, he recognises the nature of his condition: not freedom, as he had hoped, but imprisonment. He realises that the self he had

been trying to create and project is necessarily a fake because it is based on language and all language can offer is a
distorted image of the world. Words, then, do not produce
solid presence; rather, they conjure up ghosts: shadowy images of reality, neither a part of that reality, nor wholly confined to the prison of human consciousness, but something
"other". This conclusion is not the solipsistic nightmare it
might be for Banville. As Freddie says:

> When you tell the truth, that's the end of it; lies on
> the other hand, ramify in all sorts of directions,
> complicating things, knotting them up in themselves,
> thickening the texture of life. Lying makes a dull
> world more interesting. To lie is to create. (*G*, 191)

It is as near to a direct and comprehensible manifesto as a
reader is likely to get from Banville's writing as to his fundamental attitude to the process of creation itself. "To lie is to
create" and to create is to enter into a lie. Perhaps, what is
being asked of the reader is reconsider the traditional negative connotations that surround the concept of lying.

Banville's own estimation of the third book in the "art
trilogy", *Athena*, is correct: it is one book too many, stretch-
ing whatever interest a reader might have in Freddie as a
character almost to breaking point (Schwall, 1997: 13). One
aspect, though, that is of interest to this present discussion,
reconfirming the conclusion of *Ghosts*, can be observed in
the seven catalogue entries for the seven paintings central to
the text. Each painting is by a different artist whose names
are various combinations of "John Banville". Thus, the air of
playful fiction-making that pervaded *Ghosts* continues here.
What is striking about these entries, written by Freddie, is
their increasing lack of objectivity as the novel progresses.
More and more, Freddie is drawn into the act of interpreting what he sees, his comments becoming more personal
and impassioned. As was the case with Vaublin's "Le Monde

d'Or" in *Ghosts*, he begins to see himself in these works of art; they seem to encapsulate his own story and his own condition. This tells us something about what the imagination does in its engagement with the world of reality: it recreates itself in that world, finding only what it wants to find and never the thing-in-itself. The world, then, as Banville's characters perceive it, is haunted: haunted by that sense of themselves that they believe they see everywhere and in everything.

The version of Freddie Montgomery that occupied the pages of *Ghosts* declared his belief in the absolute necessity for disguise:

> To thine own self be true, they tell you; well, I allowed myself that luxury just once and look what happened. No, no, give me the mask any day, I'll settle for inauthenticity and bad faith, those things that only corrode the self and leave the world at large unmolested. (*G*, 198)

Masks, disguises and deception are now brought to the fore in John Banville's next novel, *The Untouchable* (1997). In contrast to his overt playfulness, as an author, with the slipperiness of the world of *Ghosts* where nothing was as it seemed and uncertainty held sway, Banville returns to the concrete facts of history for the source material of this novel. It is a reappearance of the method that was so successful in producing *Doctor Copernicus* and *Kepler*, books which benefited from Banville's meticulous and painstaking research into the lives of these two renaissance figures. Similar evidence of such toil can be discovered in *The Untouchable*, which has a more recent historical focus, being based as it is on the infamous Cambridge Soviet spy ring made up of figures such as Guy Burgess, Donald Maclean and Kim Philby. For an author like Banville, with his interests in deconstructing the realms of truth and fiction, and considering identity as something permanently in flux rather than being fixed and solid, the attractions of what amounts to a good old-fashioned spy thriller are obvious. Despite its origins in historical reality, the world of *The Untouchable* complements that of *Ghosts* in that it is yet another murky, unclear place with deception and double-dealing at its very centre.

The figure around which Banville focuses his fiction is based on the last of the Cambridge spies to be found out. Anthony Blunt, an art historian, was discovered as a traitor in 1979. Unlike his comrades, he had not fled to the Soviet Union but had remained in Britain and his unmasking caused great scandal, owing to his privileged position as Keeper of the Queen's Pictures. As a model for a character that might fascinate Banville, he is perfect — a man with an aesthetic sensibility coupled with a life-long adherence to the doctrine of the mask.

As would be expected, the narrative is told from the first-person perspective: Victor Maskell — the name itself is suggestive of the issues central to the novel — after his treason has been revealed, sets out to tell his own story and in so doing explain and justify his political act of betrayal. Banville, as an author, does not take too many liberties with the facts of the story and the label "faction" could be applied to *The Untouchable*, more so than it could have been to some of his previous novels which were based on real characters and events. On one level, then, this is quite a straightforward and accessible work, much more approachable from the reader's point of view than even a novel like *The Book of Evidence*. It is a welcome relief from the often knotty and difficult writing of books like *Ghosts* and *Athena*, which precede it, and yet connoisseurs of Banville's work might think that such clarity and openness is an indication of a deficiency in the novel.

There are two areas in particular where Banville does take liberties with his source material. Firstly, he has his character Maskell come from an Anglo-Irish background. He bases this aspect of his story on the early life of the poet Louis MacNeice, born in Carrickfergus in the North of Ireland, and educated in public school and in Cambridge in Britain. MacNeice actually knew Anthony Blunt but did not share his political views.

Once again the reader can observe Banville making use of Irish concerns in his writing, even in this most British of narratives. In doing so, his story of betrayal is complicated and, from an Irish vantage point, made infinitely more interesting. The most immediate consequence of grafting MacNeice's life onto that of Victor Maskell is that it exaggerates his sense of homelessness and displacement, of not fully belonging to or engaging with any of the worlds in which he finds himself located. It brings to the forefront, too, Maskell's sense of division and the incongruity of being the quintessential Englishman when, in fact, he is from Ireland. Like Oscar Wilde, who reinvented himself when he moved to Oxford from Dublin in the second half of the nineteenth century, Maskell's position and his acceptance into this world highlights how fluid and non-essential racial identity actually is. Maskell's situation is further complicated with the information that his family's origins are not simply Anglo-Irish and Protestant but are, in reality, Gaelic and Catholic:

> The west for [my father] was the land of youth . . . but [also] the place where his people had originated, mysterious autochthons stepping out of the mists of the western seaboard, the mighty O Measceoils, warriors, pirates, fierce clansmen all, who just in time to avoid the ravages of the Famine had changed their religion and Anglicised the family name and turned themselves into Yeats's hard-riding country gentlemen. (*U*, 77)

The consequences of this act from the past reverberate throughout Maskell's life, as if he is condemned to constantly re-enact this original moment of betrayal over and over again in his every act and word. In a conversation with his Soviet contact, Felix Hartmann, Maskell comments on his companion's declared lack of rootedness in his chosen life:

> "I have no home."
> "No," I said, "I suppose you haven't. I should have thought that would make you feel quite . . . free?" (*U*, 146).

That Felix chooses not to reply to this question is answer enough: freedom, yes, but at what cost? And it is not solely Felix's dilemma, but Maskell's own. His whole life becomes one of denial, of betraying his origins and, in doing so, himself. On a visit to Carrickdrum, his home, he chooses to keep his family history from his friend Nick:

> In these matters he and I observed a decorous silence: he did not speak of his Jewishness nor I of my Catholic blood. We were both, in our own ways, self-made men. (*U*, 146)

But as the main character in Banville's next novel, *Eclipse*, declares: "The self-made man has no solid ground to stand on" (*E*, 37), and is therefore doomed forever to perform and create, improvising both self and home in an ongoing effort to be. And from this, there is no rest. What is remarkable from Maskell's account is how one act of dissembling and deceit necessarily leads to another, each new lie further distancing him from the truth.

Identity being thought of as something fluid and uncertain, then, is central to Maskell's predicament as delineated in *The Untouchable*. His being Irish gives his spying career an added piquancy, as if his background prepares him for his life of double dealing, making it easier because, in truth, it is something he has always had to do. It is, too, a comment on the structured nature of identity in the Irish context and how complicated and protean a thing is Irish identity. Despite the insistent use of labels such as Protestant and Catholic, Anglo-Irish and Gaelic-Irish, these terms — as in the case of Victor Maskell — conceal as well as reveal.

The second liberty Banville takes with the original life of Anthony Blunt is that he has his Victor Maskell get married, only coming to understand his homosexuality later. Having an openly gay character is something new in Banville's fiction, though with a character like Copernicus, for example, being unable or unwilling to acknowledge this aspect of his sexuality, it is not wholly original territory for the writer. Freddie Montgomery, too, can be read in this way, with parts of his narrative subtly hinting at a gay relationship with Charlie. Here, as with Maskell's Irishness, it affords Banville the opportunity of adding another layer to his character's need for wearing a mask. The Britain presented here is one where homosexuality is illegal, thus forcing Maskell and others to exist in a gloomy underworld of illicit trysts. In a very real way, also, it highlights the thrill associated with doing what one knows is beyond the accepted norms of society. It complements his world of espionage and counter-espionage, offering those cold political acts a very human disposition.

The world of the spy offers Maskell the perfect excuse not to be himself, the burden of which is far too much for him to sustain — as it is for many of Banville's leading men. Far easier to be someone else, than to have to be yourself:

> This instability, this myriadness that the world takes on, is both the attraction and the terror of being a spy. Attraction, because in the midst of such uncertainty you are never required to be yourself; whatever you do, there is another, alternative you

> standing invisibly to one side, observing, evaluating,
> remembering. This is the secret power of the spy . . .
> it is the power to be and not to be, to detach one-
> self from oneself, to be oneself and at the same time
> another. (*U*, 143)

Thus, his Marxism is only skin-deep, another disguise to hide
conveniently behind. Though Marxist doctrine is attractive
to Maskell, or appears to be so, because of its emphasis on
action in the real world: "'We must have action,' I said, with
all the doggedness of the dogmatist. 'We must act, or per-
ish.'" (*U*, 60).

In a way, Maskell envies his comrades, like Boy
Bannister, who can seemingly act without thought or re-
serve. Boy is another of those individuals that populate Banville's books, whose very presence mocks the over-
earnestness of the hero, their ability to simply "be", a taunt
to the overly conscious and intellectual life being pursued by
the main character. This concern with action opens up an
interesting link to Louis MacNeice. In his long autobiographi-
cal poem "Autumn Journal", MacNeice deals with the problem of his various political commitments and allegiances, and
in section sixteen focuses specifically on in his Irish relationships:

> We envy men of action
> Who sleep and wake, murder and intrigue
> Without being doubtful, without being haunted.
>   (Deane, 1991: 160)

The necessity of action, then, in numerous contexts is central to Maskell's predicament.

Invariably, Maskell's attempts at action in the form of
subterfuge amount to very little. As Banville portrays him,
Maskell is not very central to the world of espionage, the
information he passes over is not of very high quality. Also,

Maskell has the feeling that his position is compromised, that another character is playing him for a fool. Thus, his spying, which is an attempt to gain some control over his life, is seriously undermined throughout the narrative as he drifts from episode to episode.

This issue of action and Maskell's Marxism offer some insights into the nature of art in the contemporary moment. As a man obsessed with art and as art historian, he has obvious interest in the approaches taken to consider the work of art. In conversations with his colleagues, he spouts the Marxist line:

> "Yes," I said, "it is the case that I did once argue for the primacy of pure form. So much in art is merely anecdotal, which is what attracts the bourgeois sentimentalist. I wanted something harsh and studied, the truly lifelike: Poussin, Cézanne, Picasso. But these new movements — this surrealism, these arid abstractions — what do they have to do with the actual world, in which men live and work and die?" (*U*, 111)

Art and the artist must enter into the world of action; must, as Maskell goes on to declare, "contribute to the great forward movement of history" (*U*, 112). Otherwise, the art descends "to the level of mere decoration and self-indulgent revery" (*U*, 113). Of course, Maskell does not believe a word of what he is proclaiming in this scene, as he later demonstrates when he tells the reader about his great work of criticism concerning the artist Nicolas Poussin:

> How I used to sneer at those critics — the Marxists especially, I am afraid — who spent their energies searching for the meaning of his work . . . The fact is, of course, there is no meaning. Significance, yes; affects; authority; mystery — magic, if you wish — but no meaning. The figures in the "Arcadia" are not pointing to some fatuous parable about mortality and

the soul and salvation; they simply are. Their meaning is that they are there. This is the fundamental fact
of artistic creation, the putting in place of something
where otherwise there would be nothing. (Why did
he paint it? — Because it was not there.) In the ever
shifting, myriad worlds through which I moved,
Poussin was the singular, unchanging, wholly authentic thing. (*U*, 343)

His difficulty with action centres on the quality of that act.
His own life and shadowy "career" of cross and double-cross
pale in comparison with Poussin's acts of artistic transformation, owing to, as he feels, the less than authentic nature of
his own creations: that is, his various masks and disguises.
Poussin's art attains a level of solidity and reality that is absent in his own life and, indeed, in the world about him.
However, this critical study of Poussin and his work is, he
believes, his finest creation. Crucially, he sees the source of
his critical prowess manifested in his realisation of Poussin:

I do not know of any other work . . . which compre-
hensively, exhaustively and — I shall dare to say it —
magisterially captures the essence of an artist and his
art as this one does. One might say, I have invented
Poussin. I frequently think this is the chief function of
the art historian, to synthesise, to concentrate, to fix
his subject, to pull together into a unity all the dispa-
rate strands of character and inspiration and
achievement that make up this singular being, the
painter at his easel. After me, Poussin is not, cannot
be, what he was before me. That is my power. I am
wholly conscious of it. (*U*, 343)

The critic is transformed into an artist in the creation of his
subject. As with previous characters in Banville's *oeuvre*,
Maskell is able to project another figure or character, but

not himself, and remains thoroughly disconnected, displaced and alienated throughout the novel.

When he is eventually caught, Maskell offers an insight into the strain of being a spy, of being constantly what you are not, even at the instant when the game is up:

> You must start acting the moment they challenge you, not when you are already in the car, with the cuffs on. Or rather, you must never stop acting . . . even when you are alone, in a locked room, with the lights off and the blankets over your head. (*U*, 371)

There is a kind of freedom in donning a mask, but in the constant necessity to convince people of its validity, something essential is lost. Victor Maskell is, therefore, another of Banville's tragic characters, set adrift in a world of betrayal and treachery, whose crime, in the end, is not simply a political one, but a personal one. He has deluded himself in the creation of a space wherein he can act, wherein he can be. Yet, the final words of the novel: "Father, the gate is open" (*U*, 405), brings to mind a moment from the past in his home of Carrickdrum: it is there, perhaps, that the real Victor is to be found, unconsciously at one with the world and with his family. The rest of his life has been lived beyond that gate in a multitude of guises. Of course, the past can never be fully recovered and memory itself is defective. So, this end is not a resolution as such, but a comfort to an old man who has lost everything, now dreaming of a time when all was well with the world and his place in it was secure. As Joseph McMinn says of the novel: "If there is any redemption in *The Untouchable*, it can only lie with the quality of that deluded imagination" (McMinn, 1999: 156).

John Banville's next novel, *Eclipse* (2000), is one of his most brilliantly realised works of art. It is so because it is not a disguised fiction in the way, for instance, that *The Untouchable* is, with its playful adherence to the thriller genre which acts as a convenient backdrop for his philosophical meditation on the nature of the self and the fictions that sustain the self. Neither is it a reincarnation of the type of world rendered in *Ghosts*, baffling the reader with its endlessly reflected reality, and cleverly undermining itself at every turn. *Eclipse* eschews such trickery in favour of a very human tale that in tone and economical execution is reminiscent of *The Newton Letter*.

Plot has always been problematical in Banville's work. He has, as has been observed, on many occasions turned to the past, both distant and more recent, to obtain "stories" that can be transformed in his own act of writing. Here, in *Eclipse*, there is very little plot to speak of and indeed the term "novel" would be inappropriately applied to what is an extended short story. It is very much a mood piece. Instead of using action, the narrative is carried along by the introspective voice of the main protagonist. The Irish novelist Elizabeth Bowen once declared that her writing was concerned with rendering "life with the lid on" (Glendinning, 1977: 73). It is an apt description to apply to Banville's writing in general, which is also fundamentally preoccupied with containment. From his early novels, his writing has been about attempting to register the complexity of the delicate fragility of the relationship between the self and the world in which it exists. His characters enter into a search for an appropriate language that will contain their experience, and render themselves and their lives knowable. He has, consequently, developed a unique style to make this process manifest: it is at once controlled and controlling, moving at times out of the realm of prose toward poetry, hinting at the deep emotions possessed by his tragic narrators.

"Life with the lid on" is a perfectly apt phrase to describe Banville's prose in general, but in particular as it is deployed in this recent work. Such a description conjures up images of violent emotion being restrained by a rigid façade of calm and order. It suggests, too, a tension between genteel outward appearance and the reality of a ferment within. And it is exactly this type of tension which infuses this novel. Without the distraction of a plot, *Eclipse* is a marvellously poised performance, at once calm yet intimating perfectly the turbulent emotions at work beneath a surface manifestation of composure.

In the novels immediately preceding *Eclipse*, Banville had toyed with the idea of acting: characters like Freddie Montgomery and Victor Maskell being presented as consummate performers, always keeping their true essential self hidden behind a variety of masks and disguises. Here, in acknowledgement of the direction in which this concept was moving, his main character and narrator, Alexander Cleave, is an actor by profession. The premise upon which the novel is structured is that he has returned to his home place in the southeast of Ireland after suffering something of a breakdown which had culminated in his drying up during a performance on stage. He ponders and mulls over his past, trying to discover the nature of what has befallen him. His life has been given over to improvising identities, losing himself in other people's words and actions, and he realises the cost of such a constant immersion in these numerous roles:

> I spoke all the parts, even of the vanquished and the slain. I would be anyone but myself. Thus it continued year on year, the intense, unending rehearsal. But what was I rehearsing for? When I searched inside myself, I found nothing finished, only a permanent potential, a waiting to go on. At the site of what was supposed to be my self was only a vacancy, an ecstatic hollow. (*E*, 33)

This fundamental absence he had hoped to transform by his studied attention to his art. He had desired to discover a "cast of characters" who would inhabit the world in a "big-

ger, grander" and more weighty fashion than he could ever
hope to do (*E*, 36). He comes to understand, though, that
what he wants — "nothing less than a total transformation,
a making-over of all I was into a miraculous, bright new being" (*E*, 37) — is beyond his powers.

In coming home, he believes he can begin to heal the rift
between his self and the world, a rift that is reflected in his
own sense of being fractured:

> Free then of all encumbrance, all distraction, I might
> be able at last to confront myself without shock or
> shrinking. For is this not what I am after, the pure
> conjunction, the union of self with sundered self? I am
> weary of division, of being always torn. I shut my eyes
> and in a sort of rapture see myself stepping backward
> slowly into the cloven shell, and the two halves of it,
> still moist with glair, closing round me. (*E*, 70)

As is always the case with Banville, names are important:
thus, both meanings of Cleave hold true in this narrative.
Alex desires both to connect with his world and to understand it, but he also has to acknowledge his utter disconnection from the world and from others in that world.

His time is taken up with documenting the minutiae of
his "new" life, shared by Quirke, the caretaker of the family
home, and Quirke's daughter Lily. These characters, and
especially their names, are suggestive of their literary ante-
cedents in, respectively, Maria Edgeworth's *Castle Rackrent*
and James Joyce's short story "The Dead" from his collection *Dubliners*. Once again, Banville gives his narrative a
haunted air with these subtle and shadowy references.
Haunting, though, is central to the text and not simply on
this literary level. Cleave is certain that the house is haunted
by a mother and child, glimpses of whom he catches momentarily when he least expects it. He is driven, in consequence, further into the past: his childhood, his marriage, his

own child Cass, are all brought to his mind as he contemplates the numerous failures that punctuate his life. He is unable to find the key that will unlock the mystery, offering instead, as one critic notes: "wonderfully vivid moments, rich in detail, but only vaguely suggestive in meaning" (d'Hoker, 2001: 21).

Knowledge gleaned from reading Banville's previous fiction should signal to the reader that this lack of narrative accuracy and coherence is exactly what Cleave is after but cannot achieve; thus the story he tells has, inherent within it, echoes of the larger predicament it is trying to express.

He no longer cares for the potential of an endless rehearsal for some future moment: he wants, as he says, "To cease becoming and merely be" (E, 77). Other people, he observes, seem to possess this state of unconscious being that he yearns for. He recalls how, when he was first married to Lydia, he used to watch a young woman dress in the apartment opposite his. Her lack of self-consciousness is fascinating to him; he feels that, because she is not aware she is being watched, she is free. It is ironic, of course, that as an actor, Cleave's "art" only comes into being when he is perceived by an audience. His problem is that he cannot do without this audience: he is nothing if he is not being watched. His interest in others is not wholly altruistic and his wife Lydia calls him a vivisectionist: "'You want to study them,' she said, 'take them apart, like a watch, to see how they work.'" (E, 160). He is unable to let things be, constantly positioning himself in order that he can gain a vantage point on the world and on others, dissecting every move and every scene and, in doing so, draining those moments of their true significance. Cleave's tragedy, for it is a tragedy (the five parts of the book echoing the classical five acts of drama), is similar to that experienced by every other character that Banville has created. The world he creates, through his close observations and the subsequent narrative that follows, has little to do with reality. What should be an act of enlightenment becomes, instead, an act of wilful blindness. This is comically underlined in a conversation with Lydia:

> "I have the feeling," I said, "the conviction, I can't rid myself of it, that something has happened, something dreadful, and I haven't taken sufficient notice, haven't paid it due regard, because I don't know what it is." . . .
>
> "Maybe it's your life," she said. "That's disaster enough, isn't it?" (*E*, 145)

His scrutinising perception seems to be always focused on the wrong object — when he is caught up in himself, it is others he should be considering; and when he observes others, it is his own self that his sights should be trained on.

There are moments when he does seem to register some understanding of his situation regarding the nature of the fault in his relationships. For instance, he recalls a time when Lydia's "otherness", her self-contained being, became forcefully apparent to him:

> Despite the absurdity of it, what I had understood in that vision of her, simply, astonishingly, was the absolute otherness, not only from me, but from everything else in the world, that was the world . . . I had conceived her, as I did so much else, to be part of me, or at least of immediate vicinity, a satellite fixed and defined within the gravitational field of the body, of the planet, of the red giant of being. (*E*, 159)

He realises that power and control are at the heart of his problem with the world in general and with those people who occupy the space in his immediate vicinity, namely his family. For all his posturing, it is only himself that he is really interested in and he does, at one stage, admit that he is a "cold-hearted bastard", recognising that he has never been able to make that leap of faith and connect fundamentally with others.

Eclipse is ostensibly concerned with the plight of Alexander Cleave but, as the novel progresses, it becomes increasingly clear that the person haunting the narrative is his daughter Cass. Cass suffers from schizophrenia and, obviously, Cleave finds some echo of his own dilemma in her condition. And yet, to a certain extent she seems able to cope with this illness and make something of her life. This the reader discovers only at the end, after her death: Cass has an academic respect and recognition that her father did not really know about, so caught up in himself has he been. He now fully comprehends the mistakes he has made and has been making all his life:

> For if I knew, if the ghosts were a premonition that this was what was to come, why did I not act? But then, I have always had the greatest difficulty distinguishing between action and acting. Besides, I was looking the wrong way, I was looking into the past, and that was not where the phantoms were from, at all. (*E*, 208)

Yet another of Banville's characters realises too late that what it is they have been searching for, was there all along, if only they cared to look.

Some reviewers of *Eclipse* made a connection between Banville's character and the author himself, suggesting that perhaps his tracing of Alexander Cleave's mid-life crisis is a reference to his own situation (d'Hoker, 2001: 21). Again and again, Banville has been at pains to stress that his is not an art concerned with self-expression; hence the scaffolding that "real" stories and historical figures offer him as a means of projecting characters and events rather than reflecting his own life and times. And yet, those novels — like *The Newton Letter*, *Mefisto* and *Ghosts*, which have no such ready-made plot upon which they depend — can be seen as more personal narratives, each focused on individual writer or artist figures whose difficulty in telling their own stories is matched by Banville's own. Perhaps in a character like Cleave, who has spent his life looking, as it were, in the wrong direction, Banville recognises his own precarious position as a writer who might have chosen the wrong subject matter. It is a courageous stance to take: at once critical of his past work, but also forward-looking in that it suggests that another book, another act of writing, is necessary in order to continue his own search for a word or set of symbols that might in some way begin to adequately express the human condition.

Chapter 5

Conclusion

Ah, this plethora of metaphors! I am like everything except myself. (*Athena*, 90)

It has become something of a convention that Irish culture is presented as one where the act of story-telling is celebrated above all else. Being the clearest remnant of a Gaelic culture which revolved round the oral tradition, stories become paramount to such an extent that the value attached to certain prose works is based solely on the nature of the story told and the expertise employed in its telling. Certainly, in the last ten or fifteen years, which has witnessed an unprecedented upsurge in the production and consumption of Irish fiction, this still holds true, as new Irish stories are told from new perspectives, widening what is the expected and accepted subject matter and terrain of the traditional Irish narrative. This present study has demonstrated how John Banville is not a storyteller in that tradition: he would seem to have no personal story to tell, nor is he interested in weaving realistic fictions documenting the harsh truths of contemporary Ireland in way that other writers, like Roddy Doyle or Dermot Bolger for instance, supposedly do.

A common criticism consequently levelled at John Banville's work is that, perhaps because of this perceived lack of interest in storytelling, it is far too intellectual and cleverly playful for its own good. The thematic approach adopted in this book has undoubtedly been sensitive to the important role that ideas play in Banville's writing. Thus, concerns about language, Irish history, art and the nature of the self in the contemporary world have been focused on and discussed. Nevertheless, the implication of this criticism is that Banville's writing amounts to a kind of sophisticated fictional gamesmanship rather than dealing with the pressures of lived experience. In other words, real emotion is replaced by a cold, calculating desire to engage only with abstract intellectual concerns.

Yet it has also been shown here that there is a story embedded in Banville's fiction: an essential narrative concerned with tracing the modern human condition of being caught in a liminal position between the poles of hope and despair. The despair stems from the recognition that an old world of unifying, grand visions, which had the potential to order and give meaning to the world and man's place in the world, are no longer possible; this is coupled with the hopeful desire that such a vision might still be attainable. It is a narrative that at once concedes the impotence of the human imagination in the face of an indifferent reality, while also celebrating the imagination that dares to continue to imagine. His is a story, therefore, that occupies an in-between space amid tense and anxious oppositions, that Janus-like looks backward and forward simultaneously, caught between tradition and modernity, ever in flux but longing for a terminal point.

There is, too, real feeling to Banville's articulation of this postmodern dilemma. Near the close of *Eclipse*, Alexander Cleave comes to some form of understanding of his situation, and offers this observation:

> The tragedians are wrong, grief has no grandeur.
> Grief is grey, it has a grey taste and grey ashy feel on
> the fingers. (*E*, 191)

As an actor intimate with the great plays of the stage, Cleave
has attempted to give his own tragedy a sense of distinction,
like the heightened tragedy that those classics texts from the
past possessed. He discovers, however, that there is no glory
in tragedy and grief, that such a transfiguration of emotion is
not actually possible in the all-too-real world he finds himself
now inhabiting. All of Banville's characters come to know, to
varying degrees, their position in this fallen world: from Copernicus to Kepler, from the unnamed narrator of *The Newton Letter* to Freddie Montgomery in his various guises.

Even when Banville steps outside his preferred medium
of fiction, the same fundamental narrative is played out. His
short television drama, *Seachange* (1994), brings a man and
woman together, by chance, on a bench at the end of a pier
by the sea. He tells his tale of being nearly drowned and his
miraculous survival. His story gains added significance because on that day a child drowned at the very same spot.
The man's incessant talking is contrasted with the silence of
the woman who is so obviously in distress. As the drama
unfolds it becomes apparent that the silent woman is the
mother of the dead child. In its brevity, *Seachange* offers a
stark, uncluttered glimpse at the deep emotion at work in
Banville's writing. It would be far too easy to interpret the
woman, in her silence, as representing the real location of
feeling in this piece. For the man, too, in his own faltering
way as he tries to come to understand what has happened
to him, embodies the pain and confusion that is our lot in
the present moment. Certainly, his chatter might seem inap-
propriate, but he is driven — like all of Banville's protagonists are driven — to give words to his thoughts, no matter
how imperfect they may be.

The major challenge for a reader coming to Banville's work is identifying the nature of this essential narrative and engaging with it through its numerous manifestations in his writing over the last 30 years. While each novel can be read and enjoyed individually, it is only in thinking of them as being parts of a whole that the reader can fully appreciate the purpose and design holding the diversity of his fictions together. That Banville is fond of working within the framework of series — the science tetralogy, the art trilogy — gives a clue to his methodology: each novel is a variation on a theme, a provisional staging-post on a yet-to-be-completed journey.

Consequently, there is a very real way in which a conclusion to a discussion of John Banville's fiction is redundant. His work as a whole, and individually, speaks for itself and all a conclusion can offer is a reiteration of what has already been said. There is another, perhaps more important, way in which a conclusion is not necessary: it imposes an artificial ending on a body of work which is still in process, evolving and mutating with each subsequent addition to it. For here lies another challenge to a reader approaching Banville's work: engaging with its radical openness, in that no end is ever finally, or definitively, reached.

Each individual chapter in this study ends on something of an upbeat note: Irish history, art, the self are all deemed problematical categories, and yet the task that Banville sets himself in the midst of these difficulties is to begin to reimagine them. He forces his readers to confront what they think they already know, to look at the world in a new way and thereby re-engage with it. Tragedy in the classical sense may no longer be possible but that should not stop him, or us, in attempting to rethink tragedy for the contemporary moment. That, for Banville, is the role for a new type of hero: to continue to search for words, symbols and fictions adequate to our predicament.

In the end, there is no "end", only endless beginnings.

Bibliography

Books by John Banville

Banville, John (1970), *Long Lankin*, Oldcastle, Co. Meath, Ireland: Gallery Press. Reprinted 1991.

Banville, John (1971), *Nightspawn*, Oldcastle: Gallery Press. Reprinted 1993.

Banville, John (1973), *Birchwood*, London: Panther Books. Reprinted 1984.

Banville, John (1976), *Doctor Copernicus*, London: Paladin. Reprinted 1987.

Banville, John (1981), *Kepler*, London: Minerva. Reprinted 1990.

Banville, John (1982), *The Newton Letter: An Interlude*, London: Secker and Warburg. Reprinted 1983.

Banville, John (1986), *Mefisto*, London: Paladin. Reprinted 1987.

Banville, John (1989), *The Book of Evidence*, London: Minerva. Reprinted 1990.

Banville, John (1993), *Ghosts*, London: Secker and Warburg.

Banville, John (1995), *Athena*, London: Secker and Warburg.

Banville, John (1997), *The Untouchable*, London: Picador.

Banville, John (2000), *Eclipse*, London: Picador.

Plays by John Banville

Banville, John (1994), *The Broken Jug*, Oldcastle: Gallery Press.

Banville, John (1994), *Seachange*, Radio Telefís Éireann.

Banville, John (2000), *God's Gift*, Oldcastle: Gallery Press.

Interviews with John Banville and Theoretical Writings

Banville, John (1981), "A Talk", *Irish Literary Supplement*, XI, 1 (Spring).

Banville, John (1990), "Survivors of Joyce" in Augustine Martin (ed.), *The Artist and the Labyrinth*, London: Ryan.

Banville, John (1993), "Making Little Monsters Walk" in Clare Boylan (ed.), *The Agony and the Ego: The Art and Strategy of Fiction Writing Explored*, London, Penguin Books.

Banville, John (2001), "The day a poker poked a hole in modern thinking: A Review of *Wittgenstein's Poker* by David Edmonds", *The Irish Times*, 26 May.

Carty, Ciaran (1986), "Out of Chaos comes Order", *The Sunday Tribune*, 14 September.

Imhof, Rüdiger (1981), "My Readers, That Small Band, Deserve a Rest", *Irish Literary Supplement*, XI, 1.

Ní Anluain, Clíodhna (2000), *Reading the Future: Irish Writers in Conversation with Mike Murphy,* Dublin: Lilliput Press.

Schwall, Hedwig (1997), "An Interview with John Banville", *The European English Messenger*, Vol. VI/1.

Sheehan, Ronan (1979), "Novelists on the Novel. Ronan Sheehan talks to John Banville and Francis Stuart", *The Crane Bag*. Vol. 3, No. 1.

Books and articles by other authors about John Banville and Other Works Cited

Beckett, Samuel (1970), *Proust & 3 Dialogues with George Duthuit*, London: John Calder Limited.

Beckett, Samuel (1979), *The Beckett Trilogy*, London: Picador.

Brown, Terence (1991), "Redeeming the Time: the Novels of John McGahern and John Banville" in James Acheson (ed.) *The British and Irish Novel since 1960*, New York: St Martin's Press.

Burgstaller, Susanne (1992), "'This Lawless House': John Banville's Post-Modernist Treatment of the Big-House Motif in *Birchwood* and *The Newton Letter*" in Otto Rauchbauer (ed.) *Ancestral Voices: The Big House in Anglo-Irish Literature: A Collection of Interpretations*, Dublin: The Lilliput Press.

Conrad, Joseph (1988), *Heart of Darkness*, London: W.W. Norton and Company.

Cronin, Gearóid (1991), "John Banville and the Subversion of the Big House Novel" in Jacqueline Genet (ed.) *The Big House in Ireland: Reality and Representation*, Dingle: Brandon.

Deane, Seamus (1985), *Celtic Revivals: Essays in Modern Irish Literature 1880–1980*, London: Faber and Faber.

Deane, Seamus (1975), "'Be Assured I Am Inventing': The Fiction of John Banville" in Patrick Rafroidi & Maurice Harmon (eds.) *The Irish Novel in Our Time*, Lille: PUL.

d'Hoker, Elke (2000), "Books of Revelation: Epiphany in John Banville's Science Tetralogy and *Birchwood*", *Irish University Review*, Vol. 30, No.1 (Spring/Summer).

d'Hoker, Elke (2001), "Cleaving as a Fine Art", *Irish Literary Supplement*, Vol. 20, No. 1.

Docherty, Thomas (1993), *A Postmodern Reader*, London: Harvester Wheatsheaf.

Donnelly, Brian (1975), "The Big House in the Recent Novel", *Studies*, 64.

Eliot, George (1987), *Middlemarch*, Harmondsworth, Middlesex: Penguin Books.

Fisk, Robert (1983), *In Time of War: Ireland, Ulster and the Price of Neutrality 1939–45*, London: Andre Deutsch.

Fitzgerald, F. Scott (1984), *The Great Gatsby*, Harmondsworth, Middlesex: Penguin Books.

Foucault, Michel (1977), *Language, Counter-Memory, Practice*, Oxford: Blackwell.

Friel, Brian (1989), *Selected Plays*, London: Faber and Faber.

Glendinning, Victoria (1977), *Elizabeth Bowen: A Biography*, New York: Avon Books.

Hand, Derek (1993), "Nearly a Novel: A Review of John Banville's *Ghosts*", *Irish Literary Supplement*, XII, 2.

Hand, Derek (1994), "Banville's *The Newton Letter*: Perfect Postmodernism", *Ropes: Review of Postgraduate Studies*, 2.

Hand, Derek (2000), "John Banville and Irish History: *The Newton Letter*" in P.J. Mathews (Editor), *New Voices in Irish Criticism*, Dublin: Four Courts Press.

Hassan, Ihab (1982), *The Dismemberment of Orpheus: Toward a Postmodern Literature*, Wisconsin: The University of Wisconsin Press.

Heaney, Seamus (1998), *Opened Ground: Poems 1966–1996*, London: Faber and Faber.

Imhof, Rüdiger (1998), *John Banville: A Critical Introduction*, Dublin: Wolfhound Press.

Joyce, James (1991), *Ulysses*, London: Penguin.

Joyce, James (1984), *A Portrait of the Artist as a Young Man*, London: Penguin.

Kearney, Richard (1988a), *The Wake of Imagination: Ideas of Creativity in Western Culture*, London: Hutchinson.

Kearney, Richard (1988b), *Transitions: Narratives in Modern Irish Culture*, Dublin: Wolfhound Press.

Koestler, Arthur (1968), *The Sleepwalkers: A History of Man's Changing Vision of the Universe*, London: Hutchinson.

Kelleher, Margaret (1997), *The Feminization of Famine: Expressions of the Inexpressible?* Cork: Cork University Press.

Kiberd, Declan (1995), *Inventing Ireland: The Literature of the Modern Nation*, London: Jonathan Cape.

Kreilkamp, Vera (1998), *The Anglo-Irish Novel and the Big House*, Syracuse, New York: Syracuse University Press.

Lernout, Geert (1988), "Banville and Being: *The Newton Letter* and History" in J. Duytzchaever and Geert Lernout (eds.) *History and Violence in Anglo-Irish Literature*, Amsterdam: Rodopi.

Lernout, Geert (1986), "Looking for Pure Visions", *Graph: Irish Literary Review*, 1.

Lysaght, Sean (1991), "Banville's Tetralogy: The Limits of Mimesis", *Irish University Review*, Vol. 21, No. 1 (Spring/Summer).

Marvell, Andrew (1967), *Selected Poetry*, New York: Signet.

McCarthy, Conor (2000), *Modernisation: Crisis and Culture in Ireland 1969–1992*, Dublin: Four Courts Press.

McCormack, David (1987), "John Banville: Literature as Criticism", *The Irish Review*, Cork University Press, No. 2.

McHale, Brian (1987), *Postmodernist Fiction*, London and New York: Routledge.

McIlroy, Brian (1992), "Reconstructing Artistic and Scientific Paradigms: John Banville's *The Newton Letter*", *Mosaic: A Journal for the Interdisciplinary Study of Literature*, Vol. 25, No. 1 (Winter).

McMinn, Joseph (1999), *The Supreme Fictions of John Banville*, Manchester: Manchester University Press.

Molloy, Francis C. (1981), "The Search for Truth: The Fiction of John Banville", *Irish University Review*, 11, 1.

O'Neill, Patrick (1990), "John Banville" in Rüdiger Imhof (ed.), *Contemporary Irish Novelists*, Tubingen: Narr.

O'Toole, Fintan (1989), "Stepping into the Limelight and the Chaos", *The Irish Times*, 21 October 1989.

Outram, Dorinda (1987), "Banville, Science and Religion: Heavenly Bodies and Logical Minds", *Graph: Irish Literary Review*, Issue 4, Dublin.

Rauchbauer, Otto (ed.) (1992), *Ancestral Voices: The Big House in Anglo-Irish Literature: A Collection of Interpretations*, Dublin: The Lilliput Press.

Smyth, Gerry (1997), *The Novel and the Nation: Studies in the New Irish Fiction*, London: Pluto Press.

Stevens, Wallace (1994), "Anecdote of the Jar" in Nina Baym et al. (eds.), *The Norton Anthology of American Literature Vol. 2*, New York and London: W.W. Norton & Company.

Swann, Joseph (1993), "Banville's Faust: *Doctor Copernicus, Kepler, The Newton Letter* and *Mefisto* as Stories of the European Mind", in Donald E. Morse et al. (eds.), *A Small Nation's Contribution to the World: Essays on Anglo-Irish Literature and Language*, Gerrards Cross: Colin Smythe.

Wilde, Oscar (1983), *The Complete Works of Oscar Wilde* with an Introduction by Vyvyan Holland, London: Collins.

Yeats, W.B. (1985), *The Collected Poems of W.B. Yeats*, London: Macmillan.

Index